D0109392

Growing Up in God's Family

BIBLE STUDY GUIDE

From the Bible-teaching ministry of

Charles R. Swindoll

INSIGHT FOR LIVING

These studies are based on the outlines of sermons delivered by Charles R. Swindoll. Chuck is a graduate of Dallas Theological Seminary and has served in pastorates for over twenty-two years, including churches in Texas, New England, and California. Since 1971 he has served as senior pastor of the First Evangelical Free Church of Fullerton, California. Chuck's radio program, "Insight for Living," began in 1979. In addition to his church and radio ministries, Chuck has authored twenty books and numerous booklets on a variety of subjects.

Chuck's outlines are expanded from the sermon transcripts and edited by Bill Watkins, a graduate of California State University at Fresno and Dallas Theological Seminary, with the assistance of Bill Butterworth, a graduate of Florida Bible College, Dallas Theological Seminary, and Florida Atlantic University. Bill Watkins is presently the director of educational resources, and Bill Butterworth is currently the director of counseling ministries at Insight for Living.

Creative Director:	Cynthia Swindoll
Editor:	Bill Watkins
Associate Editor:	Bill Butterworth
Copy Supervisor:	Wendy Jones
Editorial Assistants:	Becky Anderson and Julie Martin
Director, Communications Division:	Carla Beck
Communications Coordinator:	Alene Cooper
Art Director:	Ed Kesterson
Production Artist:	Becky Englund
Typographers:	Trina Crockett and Debbie Krumland
Calligrapher:	Richard Stumpf
Cover:	Etching by Currier and Ives, *The Four Seasons of Life: Middle Age* (1868)
Production Supervisor:	Deedee Snyder
Printer:	R. R. Donnelley & Sons Co.

An album that contains sixteen messages on eight cassettes and corresponds to this study guide may be purchased through Insight for Living, Post Office Box 4444, Fullerton, California 92634. For information, please write for the current Insight for Living catalog, or call (714) 870-9161. Canadian residents may direct their correspondence to Insight for Living Ministries, Post Office Box 2510, Vancouver, British Columbia, Canada V6B 3W7, or call (604) 272-5811.

ISBN 0-8499-8218-9

Table of Contents

Growing Up in God's Family

There is an enormous difference between growing old in the Lord and growing up *in Him. One is automatic and requires no effort at all . . . just aging. But the other is never automatic, or easy. It calls for personal discipline, continual determination, and spiritual desire. Churches are full of sleepy saints who are merely "logging time" in God's family. Where are those en route to maturity . . . the soldiers of the cross . . . the followers of the Lamb?*

These messages are designed to jolt us awake. They address some of the reasons many Christians have opted for a soft rocking chair instead of a rugged racetrack. But they represent more than strong exhortations. You will find encouragement and motivation . . . even a few how-to ideas that will turn your lethargic yawn into a smile of fresh hope.

Chuck Swindoll

Putting Truth into Action

Knowledge apart from application falls short of God's desire for His children. Knowledge must result in change and growth. Consequently, we have constructed this Bible study guide with these purposes in mind: (1) to stimulate discovery, (2) to increase understanding, and (3) to encourage application.

At the end of each lesson is a section called **Living Insights.** *There you'll be given assistance in further Bible study, thoughtful interaction, and personal appropriation. This is the place where the lesson is fitted with shoe leather for your walk through the varied experiences of life.*

In wrapping up some lessons, you'll find a unit called ***Digging Deeper.*** *It will provide you with essential information and list helpful resource materials so that you can probe further into some of the issues raised in those studies.*

It's our hope that you'll discover numerous ways to use this tool. Some useful avenues we would suggest are personal meditation, joint discovery, and discussion with your spouse, family, work associates, friends, or neighbors. The study guide is also practical for church classes and, of course, as a study aid for the "Insight for Living" radio broadcast. The individual studies can usually be completed in thirty minutes. However, some are more open-ended and could be expanded for greater depth. Their use is flexible!

In order to derive the greatest benefit from this process, we suggest that you record your responses to the lessons in a notebook where writing space is plentiful. In view of the kinds of questions asked, your notebook may become a journal filled with your many discoveries and commitments. We anticipate that you will find yourself returning to it periodically for review and encouragement.

Bill Watkins
Editor

Bill Butterworth
Associate Editor

Growing Up in God's Family

Analysis of a Crop Failure

Mark 4:1–20

Why do some people hear the good news about Jesus Christ but refuse to accept it? Why do others believe in God's Son but fail to mature in their faith? How can two people hear the same message and respond to it so differently? If we were to ask these questions of a number of people, we would most likely receive divergent responses. But this fact should not discourage us from seeking the correct answers to these queries. We will discover them in the Gospel of Mark 4:1–20. What we unearth in this passage may be disturbing to some. But we will become more effective in the evangelistic task and more productive in Christian growth when we clearly understand the message of this text and honestly respond to its truth.

I. A Few Words about the Setting

As we begin reading Mark 4, we find Jesus teaching a large crowd. In fact, the group of people listening to Him has grown to such a great number that He has resorted to using a boat anchored just offshore as His lectern (v. 1). The text goes on to say that Jesus "was teaching them many things in parables" (v. 2a). New Testament scholar Walter W. Wessel explains the nature of a parable in this way:

> The Sunday School definition of a parable—"an earthly story with a heavenly meaning"—is good as far as it goes. Many parables are stories taken out of ordinary life, used to drive home a spiritual or moral truth. But they are not always stories. Sometimes they are brief similes, comparisons, analogies, or even proverbial sayings. The Greek word *parabolé* (lit., "something placed along side [*sic*]") includes all these meanings.[1]

Furthermore, unlike allegories, in which even minute details have symbolic meanings, parables are designed to communicate one

1. Walter W. Wessel, "Mark," in *The Expositor's Bible Commentary,* 12 vols., edited by Frank E. Gaebelein (Grand Rapids: Regency Reference Library, Zondervan Publishing House, 1984), vol. 8, p. 647.

main point. Certainly, parables may convey more than one thought, but each secondary idea will directly relate to the primary one.[2]

II. A Close Look at the Parable

In this chapter Jesus gives some of His instruction through a parable. Let's examine the details of this story. Christ begins by telling His audience about a farmer who went out to his unplowed field to sow some seed (Mark 4:3). As this farmer scattered the seed, he threw some of it along the pathway that cut through his field (v. 4a; cf. 2:23). But this ground was so hard that the seed could not penetrate it. Consequently, " 'the birds came and ate it up' " (4:4b). Other seed that this farmer tossed about " 'fell on the rocky ground where it did not have much soil' " (v. 5a). The phrase "rocky ground" refers to a shelf of limestone that lay just beneath the surface of the soil. Therefore, the seed that landed on this shallow ground began to grow immediately. But " 'after the sun had risen, [the new growth] was scorched; and because it had no root, it withered away' " (vv. 5b–6). Still " 'other seed fell among the thorns, and the thorns came up and choked it, and it yielded no crop' " (v. 7). Finally, " 'other seeds fell into the good soil and as they grew up and increased, they yielded a crop and produced thirty, sixty, and a hundredfold' " (v. 8). At the close of His story, Jesus exhorts His audience to heed its message: " 'He who has ears to hear, let him hear' " (v. 9).

III. An Accurate Interpretation of the Story

Now that we have an understanding of the parable's details, we need to ascertain its spiritual meaning. Fortunately, we do not need to speculate about this, since Jesus unveils the interpretation in Mark 4:14–20. Let's explore what He has to say.

A. The sower and the seed. Jesus states that the farmer in the parable symbolizes a messenger of God, and that the seed refers to His gospel. Thus Christ and any other sower of the divine Word is in view here (v. 14; cf. 1:15, 2:2, 6:7–12; Matt. 13:19a).

B. The soil and the crop. The rest of Jesus' explanation of this parable focuses on the kinds of reception given to the gospel. As He describes four common responses to the Word, He provides the answer to our opening questions—namely, that

2. If you would like to learn more about parables and Christ's use of them during His earthly ministry, we would encourage you to consult the following sources: *The Parables and Metaphors of Our Lord,* by George Campbell Morgan (Westwood: Fleming H. Revell Co., 1943); *Windows on the Parables,* by Warren W. Wiersbe (Wheaton: Victor Books, 1979); *Poet and Peasant* and *Through Peasant Eyes: A Literary-Cultural Approach to the Parables of Luke,* by Kenneth E. Bailey, combined edition (Grand Rapids: William B. Eerdmans Publishing Co., 1983); "Parable, Allegory, Proverb," by Carl Heinz Peisker and Colin Brown, in *The New International Dictionary of New Testament Theology,* 3 vols., edited by Colin Brown (Grand Rapids: Zondervan Publishing House, 1976), vol. 2, pp. 743–56.

individuals respond differently to the same message because the condition of their wills varies.

1. **The unresponsive will.** Jesus says, " 'These are the ones who are beside the road where the word is sown; and when they hear, immediately Satan comes and takes away the word which has been sown in them' " (Mark 4:15). Some people's hearts are so cold that when they hear the plan of salvation they respond to it with complete indifference. This gives Satan the opportunity to rob them of the saving benefits of the gospel.
2. **The impulsive will.** Christ adds that a similar response arises from " 'the ones on whom seed was sown on the rocky places, who, when they hear the word, immediately receive it with joy; and they have no firm root in themselves, but are only temporary; then when affliction or persecution arises because of the word, immediately they fall away' " (vv. 16–17). These are individuals who hear the salvation message and respond to it on a purely emotional level. They may get excited about the gospel, but they do not embrace it with the conviction that allows it to take root in their hearts. Therefore, when their "faith" is tested by trials or persecution, it is exposed as being empty. In other words, hard times unmask impulsive "believers," demonstrating that their faith is not genuine. These people are just as lost as those who respond with indifference to the Word of grace.
3. **The preoccupied will.** Continuing, Jesus states that " 'the ones on whom seed was sown among the thorns . . . are the ones who have heard the word, and the worries of the world, and the deceitfulness of riches, and the desires for other things enter in and choke the word, and it becomes unfruitful' " (vv. 18–19). These hearers are probably believers who fail to grow spiritually because of their divided interests. Rather than manifest the marks of Christian maturity, they display lifestyles of carnality. One New Testament exegete explains what hinders these Christians from living productively:

> At first they seem to make good progress [in the Christian life], but the word is choked out by "the worries of this life" (v. 19)—a reference to whatever distracts people from the really important things . . . ; by "the deceitfulness of wealth"—deceitful because it gives to its possessor a false sense of security . . . ; and "the desires for other things"—an all-inclusive statement that includes everything that would choke

out the sown word and prevent it from being productive.[3]

4. **The submissive will.** The final group of hearers Jesus describes is composed of those who " 'hear the word and accept it, and bear fruit, thirty, sixty, and a hundredfold' " (v. 20). These believers are neither unresponsive, impulsive, nor preoccupied. They receive the Word gladly and seek to obey it fully. And as a result, they live fruitful Christian lives.

IV. An Honest Response to the Message

The Parable of the Sower presents a message that applies to us all. Into which category of hearers do you fall? Are you unresponsive to God's Word? If so, ask the Lord to soften your heart so that you can find everlasting life in His Son, Jesus Christ. Maybe you have accepted the Word impulsively or are riding on your emotions rather than relying on God by faith. If this is the case, you need to place your trust in Christ before salvation can be yours. Perhaps you are a Christian but are preoccupied with matters that leave you spiritually immature and unproductive. For you, godliness and its benefits will remain elusive until you confess your sin and begin eradicating the "thorns" in your life that are stifling your Christian growth. Of course, this change can occur only with God's help. So you must put yourself in His care and commit yourself to cooperating with Him in the development process. Now, if you are one of the truly submissive believers, keep pressing forward. Your reward will be great not only in this life but also in the one to come (see 1 Cor. 3:10–14, 9:24–27; 2 Cor. 4:7–18; 1 Thess. 2:19–20; 2 Tim. 4:7–8; James 1:12; 1 Pet. 5:1–5).[4]

Living Insights

Study One

This lesson revolves around the Parable of the Sower. Let's take some time to study this story in more detail.

- Turn to Mark 4:1–20. Read the passage, then try your hand at writing out the parable *in your own words.* This exercise will provide you with the opportunity to uncover the meanings of the words and the message of the story.

3. Wessell, "Mark," in *The Expositor's Bible Commentary,* vol. 8, p. 651.

4. A fuller discussion on the rewards God gives to faithful Christians may be found in the book *Improving Your Serve: The Art of Unselfish Living,* by Charles R. Swindoll (Waco: Word Books, 1981), chap. 13; and the corresponding study guide titled *Improving Your Serve,* rev. ed., edited by Bill Watkins, from the Bible-teaching ministry of Charles R. Swindoll (Fullerton: Insight for Living, 1986), pp. 76–79.

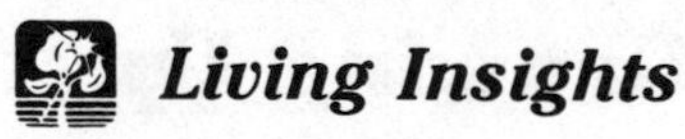

Study Two

This lesson sets the stage for our look at the ages and stages of growing up. Let's zero in on our own situation in order to apply this subject personally.

- Which soil characterizes me?
  —Am I like hardened soil beside the road . . . unresponsive to God's Word?
  —Am I like rocky soil . . . impulsive and in need of genuine faith in Christ?
  —Am I like thorny soil . . . preoccupied and in need of fully committing myself to Christ?
  —Am I like good soil . . . productive in my service to Christ?
- If I am not like the good soil, what do I need to do in order to bear spiritual fruit?

Ages and Stages of Growing Up

Selected Scripture

People often use word pictures to convey certain aspects of church life. Some liken the local congregation to a business, farm, or team. Others compare it to a school or hospital. The Bible, however, uses none of these analogies to describe an assembly. Instead, the Scriptures compare it to a *family.* And since a church is like a family, it stands to reason that a congregation goes through definite ages and stages as it progresses toward maturity. In fact, the same can be said of individual believers. Once they are born into God's forever family, they are encouraged to grow from spiritual infancy to Christian adulthood. In this lesson we will learn about the maturing process designed for and experienced both by local churches and by individual Christians. This information will encourage spiritual growth when we apply it to our lives and the assemblies in which we worship.

I. Maturity Defined

Before we talk about spiritual growth, we need to understand what it means to be a mature Christian. A grown-up believer displays wisdom, self-discipline, and commitment to a consistent walk with Christ. He or she is determined to obey God regardless of the cost and to seek regular nourishment from His Word. Also, the mature Christian strives to reach out and care for others, whether they be friend or foe, believer or unbeliever. Such an individual willingly shoulders his or her responsibilities with a contagiously positive attitude. This is what it means to be a spiritual adult. And this is the goal that all Christians and churches should strive to meet, with God's all-sufficient strength.

II. The Church as a Family

When the New Testament talks about the Church universal, it usually refers to it as the Body of Christ (cf. 1 Cor. 12:12–27). However, when the Scriptures narrow their focus to the local church, they commonly compare it to a family. Let's take a few moments to examine some of the biblical texts that use this analogy and then consider their practical significance.

A. Some scriptural support. Although there are no verses that directly connect the word *family* with the church, there are numerous instances where local assemblies are compared to or described in terms of a family unit. For example, 1 Timothy 3:4–5 says that an overseer "must be one who manages his own household well, keeping his children under control with all dignity (but if a man does not know how to manage his own household, how will he take care of the church of God?)." This qualification for the highest leadership position in the church shows us the likeness between a local assembly and a family. If a candidate needs to be a good manager of his home, then the church must resemble a family more than a business, team, or school. To this truth, Romans 8 adds these words:

> For all who are being led by the Spirit of God, these are *sons* of God. For you have not received a spirit of slavery leading to fear again, but you have received a spirit of *adoption as sons* by which we cry out, *"Abba* [Daddy]! *Father!"* The Spirit Himself bears witness with our spirit that we are *children* of God, and if *children, heirs* also, *heirs* of God and *fellow heirs* with Christ, if indeed we suffer with Him in order that we may also be glorified with Him. (Rom. 8:14–17, emphasis added)

In another passage of Scripture, we are even told to deal with fellow believers as if they were members of our natural families (1 Tim. 5:1–2). These and many other biblical examples demonstrate that the Lord views local churches as families.

B. The practical significance. We can draw at least three relevant principles from the Bible's portrayal of the church as a family. First, *because Christians are family, they should not treat one another as isolated strangers.* Cliquishness, prejudice, and disinterest should not characterize the relationships between believers. Second, *because Christians are family, they should relate to one another as loving family members do.* In other words, Christians should be caring and compassionate toward one another. They should also willingly accept the responsibility to consistently uphold their spiritual family's name, which is derived from God the Father (see Eph. 3:14–15). Third, *because Christians are family, they are responsible for their own growth toward maturity.* Just as parents cannot force their children to become responsible adults, so believers cannot make one another become mature in Christ. Spiritual maturity is an individual responsibility that each of us must accept.

III. The Stages of a Family

With these thoughts in mind, let's get an overview of the various stages that both natural and spiritual families go through.

A. Birth and infancy. When individuals become Christians, they are like "newborn babes" (cf. 1 Pet. 2:2, John 3:3, Heb. 5:12–23) —immature, fragile, greatly dependent, and extremely undiscerning. At this stage, their cry is "Help me!" Protection, patience, and an abundance of attention are desperately needed by spiritual infants.

B. Childhood and discovery. Once new believers begin taking steps on their own, they enter spiritual childhood. This is a period of learning and developing the basics of Christian doctrine and godly living. It's a very impressionable and inquisitive age that says "Tell me!" It is also a stage in which rules are eagerly sought and mildly tested.

C. Adolescence and irresponsibility. As Christians grow less dependent on others and begin to walk more boldly on their own, they move into spiritual adolescence. This period is usually marked by ambivalence, extremism, and resistance. Unfounded opinion flows freely, and the exercise of biblical wisdom sinks to a low ebb. The pervading attitude is "Show me!" and the primary focus is on self.

D. Adulthood and maturity. Lessons learned in adolescence help bring about greater stability and productivity in one's walk with God. The outcome of this is a period when self-discipline, responsiveness, responsibility, resilience, and resourcefulness dominate a Christian's approach to life. As a result, the godly adult can say to spiritually younger Christians, "Follow me!" This stage of growth is the goal of both the Christian's and the church's life. The Apostle Paul conveys this fact with these inspired words:

> And He gave some as apostles, and some as prophets, and some as evangelists, and some as pastors and teachers, for the equipping of the saints for the work of service, to the building up of the body of Christ; until we all attain to the unity of the faith, and of the knowledge of the Son of God, to a mature man, to the measure of the stature which belongs to the fulness of Christ. As a result, we are no longer to be children, tossed here and there by waves, and carried about by every wind of doctrine, by the trickery of men, by craftiness in deceitful scheming; but speaking the truth in love, we are to grow up in all aspects into Him, who is the head, even Christ, from whom the whole body, being fitted and held together by that which every joint supplies, according to the proper working of each individual part, causes the growth of the body for the building up of itself in love. (Eph. 4:11–16)

IV. Some Issues Family Members Must Face

We who have been saved by God's grace and exhorted to grow up in Christ need to honestly confront these pertinent issues and the questions they raise.

A. Identification. At which stage of spiritual growth are you? Are you a newborn babe, an inquisitive child, an unruly teenager, or a mature adult?

B. Change. What will it take to dislodge you from your present stage and accelerate your growth toward maturity? Are there some sinful habits you need to break, some "friends" you ought to drop, or some excuses you should lay to rest?

C. Urgency. When do you plan to initiate change? Are you going to procrastinate, or are you going to renew your commitment to Christian growth today?

Living Insights

Study One

As we have seen, the Scriptures use the metaphor of a family to communicate numerous truths and exhortations concerning our personal and corporate lives. Let's take this opportunity to consider some of these biblical texts.

- Make a copy of the following chart in your notebook, then carefully read each reference listed. As you do, jot down in the right column what each passage teaches about growing up in God's family and relating to its members. Your discoveries may be enlightening.

The Church As a Family	
References	Observations
John 3:3 Romans 8:14–17 Ephesians 4:11–16 1 Timothy 3:1–5 1 Timothy 5:1–2 Hebrews 5:11–14 1 Peter 2:2	

Continued on next page

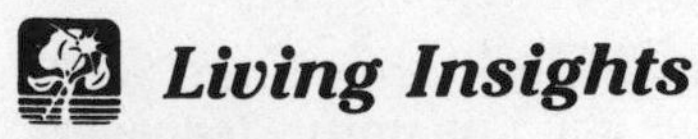

Study Two

We can rephrase the biblical admonition "Let us press on to maturity" in this way: "Let's grow up!" This exhortation raises three basic questions. They are restated below in the first person for the sake of application. Copy them into your notebook and take some time to answer them honestly.

—At which stage of spiritual growth am I?

—What will it take to dislodge me from my present stage and accelerate my growth to full maturity?

—When is the best time for me to begin?

Birth and Infancy: Operation Survival

Selected Scripture

Few things hold more excitement than the birth and infancy of a child. Although the care of a young baby can be exhausting, the special joys an infant brings usually make the child-rearing task delightful and rewarding. But the infancy stage is not without hazard. Because newborns are so fragile and dependent, their lives often hang perilously close to danger and death. What is true of physical infants is also true of spiritual babes and young congregations. Even though the needs of baby Christians are great, their potential for growth is nothing short of remarkable. These facts might prompt one to ask, How does spiritual birth begin? What is it like to be a newborn Christian? What are some of the perils of Christian infancy? How can a baby believer survive these years on his or her way to spiritual adulthood? These are the questions we will answer in this lesson. So let's see what Operation Survival is all about and discover how it applies to us.

I. The Place We Must Begin

If we want to grow up in God's forever family, we must start at the beginning—birth and infancy. Let's examine these steps more closely.

A. The necessity of birth. The Apostle John tells us how we can become children of God. Speaking about Christ, John writes, "He came to His own [things], and those who were His own did not receive Him" (John 1:11). When the Son of God descended to earth in order to take on human flesh, He came among His own creation. However, many people rejected His offer of salvation. "But as many as received Him, to them He gave the right to become children of God, even to those who believe in His name, who were born not of blood, nor of the will of the flesh, nor of the will of man, but of God" (vv. 12–13). Those who believe by faith in Christ as their Savior are delivered from spiritual death and born into God's everlasting family. This spiritual birth cannot be produced by any natural method. Rather, it is a supernatural work that God performs in response to personal faith in His Son. Jesus presented this truth to Nicodemus, saying, " 'Truly, truly, I say to you, unless one is born again [or, from above], he cannot see the kingdom of God' " (3:3). But Nicodemus misunderstood Jesus, thinking that He was speaking about a physical rebirth (v. 4). So Christ explained, " 'Truly, truly, I say to you, unless one is born of water and the Spirit, he cannot enter into the kingdom of God. That which is born of the flesh is flesh, and that which is born of the Spirit is spirit. Do not marvel that I said to you, "You must be born [from above]" ' " (vv. 5–7).

B. The reality of infancy. Spiritual infancy begins when a person is born into God's family. Christ expressed this fact in these words: " 'Truly I say to you, unless you are converted [i.e., born from above] and become like children [i.e., spiritual infants], you shall not enter the kingdom of heaven' " (Matt. 18:3). Spiritual childhood begins with humility before, and dependency on, the Lord (v. 4). Furthermore, just as physical newborns need a liquid diet during their early stages of growth, so do spiritual babes. The Apostle Peter makes this clear: "Therefore, putting aside all malice and all guile and hypocrisy and envy and all slander, like newborn babes, long for the pure milk of the word, that by it you may grow in respect to salvation, if you have tasted the kindness of the Lord" (1 Pet. 2:1–3). Baby Christians need to drink often of the pure milk of God's Word. They need to learn and apply the ABC's of the Christian faith before they are ready to handle the meatier doctrines and principles of divine revelation (cf. 1 Cor. 3:1–3a, Heb. 5:11–6:3). What is true of newborn believers is also true of infant congregations. The first local church in history began with about three thousand new converts (Acts 2:40–41). How did they survive and grow? The text tells us that they "continually [devoted] themselves to the apostles' teaching and to fellowship, to the breaking of bread and to prayer" (v. 42). They also spent a good deal of time together and sacrificially shared "their property and possessions" with anyone among them who was in need (vv. 44–46). With contagious commitment such as this, it's little wonder that the Lord added new believers to their ranks "day by day" (v. 47).

II. The Lifestyle of the Newborn

The infancy stage of a believer can be a tremendously exciting time. Frequently, the most rapid spiritual growth occurs during this period. New believers can enjoy the uncomplicated innocence of a new life in Christ. And they often have little trouble trusting others and unveiling their lives to them. But newborn Christians also have many needs. They require a great deal of time and patience from more mature believers. They need almost constant supervision in the form of discipleship as well as clear instruction in the basics of the Christian faith. They also require help in the avoidance of certain perils that are common to spiritual babes. For example, infant believers have practically no sense of discernment; they lack awareness concerning the dangers that could thwart their growth in Christ. Consequently, baby believers need the wisdom of mature

Christians to help guide them in their relationship with God and ease them into the wider responsibilities of ministry.

III. Some Essentials for Surviving Infancy

Given what we have discovered about spiritual babes, we can see that at least four things are required to help a newborn believer grow through infancy and on to childhood. If you are an infant believer, seek out Christians who can help provide you with these essentials. If you are a mature believer, take some time to promote these basics in the lives of those who are less grown-up in the faith.

A. Affection and affirmation. Like newborn infants, baby Christians need a great deal of care and encouragement for proper growth. Indeed, if they are *shown* sacrificial love, they will be more apt to express it to those with whom they come in contact.

B. Basic doctrine and a balanced lifestyle. Young believers must be grounded in the fundamental truths of the Christian faith so that they will not be "carried about by every wind of doctrine, by the trickery of men, by craftiness in deceitful scheming" (Eph. 4:14b). They also need to be shown how to apply biblical doctrine accurately and consistently so that they can reap the many benefits of a balanced Christian life.

C. Compassion and courtesy. Spiritual babes make a number of mistakes and frequently fall prey to temptation. When this occurs, they need understanding and mercy, not rejection and judgment.

D. Diet of biblical nourishment. There is no better food for infant Christians than the milk of God's life-enriching Word. As they partake of it regularly with the guidance of mature Christians, they will grow into the spiritual adults God wants them to become.

Living Insights

Study One

In this series we are comparing the physical growth of human beings to the spiritual growth of believers. Let's begin by giving some thought to the first stage—birth and infancy.

- Make a copy of the following chart in your notebook. In the middle column, write down words, phrases, or statements from the passages that describe *spiritual* birth and infancy. Then, in the right-hand column, list the traits of *physical* birth and infancy found in each passage, in order to highlight the comparison.

Continued on next page

Birth and Infancy—Operation Survival		
Passages	Spiritual Birth and Infancy	Physical Birth and Infancy
John 1:11–13		
John 3:1–7		
1 Peter 2:1–3		
Hebrews 5:11–14		

Living Insights

Study Two

The essentials for surviving spiritual infancy are vital to every stage of our Christian life. So let's use this time for some helpful self-evaluation. Think of this exercise as an opportunity to fill out your own report card. Next to each essential quality, give yourself a grade—A, B, C, etc.—and, like a good teacher, explain the reasoning for the grade. Then write out some specific steps you can take to improve your grade in each of the seven areas.

STUDENT GRADE REPORT

SUBJECTS	GRADES	REMARKS
Affection		
Affirmation		
Basic Doctrine		
Balanced Lifestyle		
Compassion		
Courtesy		
Diet of Biblical Nourishment		

GRADING SYSTEM

A—Excellent B—Above average C—Average D—Below average F—Fail

Digging Deeper

" 'Truly, truly, I say to you, unless one is born of water and the Spirit, he cannot enter the kingdom of God' " (John 3:5). This passage and others have prompted some people to conclude that water baptism is necessary for salvation (cf. Mark 16:16, Acts 2:38, Titus 3:5, 1 Pet. 3:21). But when this viewpoint is judged in light of the full teaching of Scripture concerning salvation, it cannot be validated. For example, the Bible clearly states that one is saved by faith alone (John 3:14–16, 6:40; Acts 10:43, 11:15–17, 21, 16:31, 18:8; Rom. 10:9–13; Eph. 2:8–9). The Scriptures also inform us that some of the early Christians were not baptized (Luke 23:39–43). Furthermore, the very contexts of biblical passages used to support the necessity of water baptism for salvation do not give credence to this position. For instance, in John 3:5 the Greek word translated *Spirit* can also be rendered *wind.* Both water and wind (or breath) are common symbols in Scripture for the Holy Spirit and His ministry (cf. Isa. 44:3–4; Ezek. 36:25–27, 37:9–14, 39:29; Joel 2:28–29; Acts 2:17, 33; Titus 3:5–6). Even in the Gospel of John, Jesus clearly relates the life-giving work of the Holy Spirit to wind and water (John 3:8, 7:37–39). Given these facts, it seems best to interpret *water* and *wind* in John 3:5 as symbols of God's Spirit. In other words, Christ is saying that when people place their trust in Him as their Savior (v. 16), they are born anew through the power of the Holy Spirit. Another passage which only appears to contradict salvation by faith alone is Mark 16:16. Since this passage teaches that unbelief, not the failure to observe water baptism, is the basis for condemnation, it follows that belief must be the only means of salvation. Acts 2:38 also does not support the necessity of water baptism for salvation. In the original Greek text, the imperative translated *repent* and the possessive pronoun *your* are both plural, indicating that they belong together. The command rendered *be baptized* is singular, demonstrating that it stands alone in the passage as a parenthetical thought. Consequently, the verse would be better translated this way: " 'Repent for the forgiveness of your sins; and you shall receive the gift of the Holy Spirit; and let each of you be baptized in the name of Jesus Christ.' " This rendering is confirmed by verse 41, which states that those who repented of their sins through Jesus Christ were baptized *following,* not preceding, their conversion. Contrary to the teaching of some individuals, Titus 3:5 and 1 Peter 3:21 both support the position of salvation by faith alone. The verse in Titus says that we are not saved on the basis of any works we could perform but on the basis of God's mercy by means of the Holy Spirit's regenerating and renewing power. Water baptism is not even alluded to in these verses. And the passage in 1 Peter explicitly disavows that water baptism has anything to do with being saved (cf. 1:23, Acts 15:8–9, Heb. 9:14). With this information in mind, we might ask, What is the role of water baptism in relationship to salvation by faith alone? Theologian Robert L. Saucy answers this well:

> The many instances where faith alone is mentioned without baptism as the condition of salvation make it impossible to accept any doctrine of baptismal regeneration whereby baptism is necessary for salvation. The blessings of the gospel are received through faith. Nevertheless, when that saving faith goes on to be expressed in an objective manner through baptism, God uses this act to confirm the realities of salvation. The faith of the individual is strengthened as it is openly expressed, and the saving acts of salvation are sealed and ratified with additional force to the heart of the believer.[1]

If you would like to learn more about water baptism and its relationship to salvation, we recommend that you consult the sources listed below.

- **Sources on Water Baptism**

Bates, William H. " 'Born of Water.' " *Bibliotheca Sacra* 85:338 (April 1928), pp. 230–36.

Beasley-Murray, G.R. "Baptism, Wash." In *The New International Dictionary of New Testament Theology.* 3 vols. 1st English ed. Grand Rapids: Zondervan Publishing House, 1975, 1976, 1978. Vol. 1, pp. 143–50.

Bromiley, G.W. "Baptismal Regeneration." In *The International Standard Bible Encyclopedia.* 4 vols. Rev. ed. Grand Rapids: William B. Eerdmans Publishing Co., 1979, 1982. Vol. 1, pp. 428–29.

Bromiley, G.W. et al. "Baptism." In *The International Standard Bible Encyclopedia.* Vol. 1, pp. 410–26.

Carson, Alexander. *Baptism, Its Mode and Its Subjects.* Reprint. Grand Rapids: Baker Book House, 1957.

Hodges, Zane C. "Water and Spirit—John 3:5." *Bibliotheca Sacra* 135:539 (July–September 1978), pp. 206–20.

Howard, James Keir. *New Testament Baptism.* London: Pickering and Inglis, 1970.

Marshall, I. Howard. "The Meaning of the Verb 'to baptize.' " *The Evangelical Quarterly* 45:3 (July–September 1973), pp. 130–40.

Saucy, Robert L. *The Church in God's Program.* Chicago: Moody Press, 1972. Chap. 9.

Ward, Wayne E. "Baptism in Theological Perspective." *Review and Expositor* 65:1 (Winter 1968), pp. 43–52.

1. Robert L. Saucy, *The Church in God's Program* (Chicago: Moody Press, 1972), p. 198.

Let's Return to the Basics

Selected Scripture

Spiritually speaking, the church is constantly involved in obstetrics and pediatrics. The vital local congregation is concerned that people have both a healthy birth into God's family and a consistent, balanced growth into Christian adulthood. But even the best church cannot compel people to believe in Christ and mature in the faith. Certainly, local assemblies are responsible for providing an atmosphere that encourages proselytizing and discipling (Eph. 4:11–16). However, individuals must be willing to change and grow before salvation and sanctification can become realities in their lives. Have you allowed God to begin His life-changing work in you? If you are a newborn in God's family, you need to take hold of the building blocks of Christianity in order to lay a solid foundation for your spiritual development. And even if you have passed the infancy stage, you too can benefit from a reminder of the importance of Christianity's fundamentals. So let's take this opportunity to return to the basics.

I. A Reminder of the Stages of Christian Growth

As we have already seen, there are four stages of spiritual growth. We can summarize them in the following chart:

Stages	Statements	Focus
1. Birth and Infancy	"Help me!"	Survival
2. Childhood and Discovery	"Tell me!"	Learning
3. Adolescence and Irresponsibility	"Show me!"	Challenging
4. Adulthood and Maturity	"Follow me!"	Serving

Just as we cannot skip any of these stages on the physical plane, so we cannot skip them on the spiritual level. All of us must experience each of these periods on our way to Christian maturity. However, we need to avoid becoming lodged in one of the first three because of our ignorance or stubbornness. God's desire is that we become all we can be in Christ. As the Apostle Paul points out, the Lord has given His people various gifts "for the equipping of the saints for the work of service, to the building up of the body of Christ; until we all attain to the unity of the faith, and of the knowledge of the Son of God, to a mature man, to the measure of the stature which belongs to the fulness of Christ" (Eph. 4:12–13).

II. A Return to the Basics of Spiritual Birth and Infancy

Let's zero in on the first stage of spiritual growth—birth and infancy. As we do this, we will focus on the fundamentals of each segment of this period.

A. The basics of birth. There are at least four essentials of spiritual birth that we need to understand and face.

1. **Spiritual birth is from above.** God the Father causes one "to be born again to a living hope through the resurrection of Jesus Christ from the dead" (1 Pet. 1:3). Although *God* is the *source* of salvation, *faith* in Jesus Christ is the *means* by which He actualizes salvation in a person's life (v. 9; cf. Rom. 3:21–28, Eph. 2:8–9). When individuals accept Christ as their Savior, God redeems them—He purchases them from the slave market of sin and frees them to live in obedience to Him (Rom. 6:16–23, 1 Pet. 1:14–19). Jesus confirmed these truths when He told Nicodemus, the well-known teacher of Jewish law, that he had to be " 'born again [or born from above]' " before he could be saved (John 3:3). Christ explained to him that this would occur when he chose to believe in God's " 'only begotten Son' " (v. 16).
2. **Spiritual birth must be biblical.** Educational degrees, church attendance, benevolent deeds, obedience to moral codes—none of these is mentioned in Scripture as a means of obtaining everlasting life. According to God's Word, we can do nothing to earn salvation (Gal. 2:16). Neither can we find freedom from sin in anyone other than Jesus Christ (John 14:6, Acts 4:10–12). Therefore, if we want to live forever with God and reap His abundant blessings, we must come to Him, His way.
3. **Spiritual birth must be personal.** No one can place faith in Christ for us. Neither can we inherit someone else's faith. The Lord calls on each of us to accept His salvation plan.
4. **Spiritual birth must be authentic.** We cannot be saved by merely reciting a formula, saying a prayer, or assenting to the truth. Freedom from the penalty of sin comes only when we surrender our lives to God by depending on the death of Christ as sufficient payment for all our wrongdoing (Mark 8:34–35, Heb. 10:10–18).

B. The basics of infancy. Once we are born into God's family, we become spiritual infants in need of knowing how to grow. Among the many elements that are necessary for healthy Christian growth, four are prominent.

1. **Obedience.** The Apostle Peter exhorts us to become "as obedient children" in our walk with God (1 Pet. 1:14a). We are to heed the Lord's commands as a respectful child obeys his parents. This involves refusing to become "conformed to the former lusts which were [ours] in [our] ignorance" and being willing to pursue holiness "in all [our] behavior" (vv. 14b–15).

2. **Nourishment.** Peter goes on to tell us to put "aside all malice and all guile and hypocrisy and envy and all slander, [and] like newborn babes, long for the pure milk of the word, that by it [we] may grow in respect to salvation" (2:1–2). Christian growth requires proper spiritual nourishment—the Bible. We must regularly read, study, and apply God's Word if we are going to become mature members of His family. For many of us, this might necessitate cutting down on or completely cutting out some activities. But doing so would be a small sacrifice to make in comparison to the benefits of consistently spending time in the Scriptures.
3. **Prayer.** Furthermore, we are to "be of sound judgment and sober spirit for the purpose of prayer" (4:7). One of the best ways to become acquainted with someone is to spend time talking with him or her. The same holds true in our relationship with God. We need to enter His presence often, offering our praises, petitions, and intercessions to Him through prayer. As we do, we will find our knowledge of Him growing and our intimacy with Him deepening.
4. **Spirit-filled life.** The Holy Spirit is the member of the Godhead who empowers believers to grow in the Christian faith (Rom. 8:12–27, 1 Cor. 12:4–11). He does not produce instant maturity. But infant believers will experience a more constant growth as they yield to the ministry of God's Spirit in their lives.

III. Some Questions for All to Answer

As we reflect on this lesson, we can see that there are at least two questions each of us needs to answer.

A. Have I been born from above? If not, take the opportunity now to place your trust in Christ as your Redeemer.

B. Have I mastered the steps of spiritual babyhood? If not, return to the basics so that you can begin your growth toward Christian adulthood.

Living Insights

Study One

Some of the building blocks of Christianity are revealed in the answer to the question, How does one become a Christian? The best way to answer this is to go directly to God's Word.

- One of the most foundational books in the Bible is the Gospel of John. Let's use our time together to read as much of it as time allows. You may be surprised at how quickly you move through its twenty-one chapters! In order to better understand this book, keep in mind its key concept—belief. It might be helpful to circle the words *believe, believes* and *belief* as you read along. After you finish the book, don't forget to answer the question that prompted this exercise: How does one become a Christian?

Living Insights

Study Two

We learned in this study that the church is constantly involved in spiritual obstetrics and pediatrics. Christians need to help people have a healthy *birth* into God's family and provide for their balanced *growth*. In light of this, take a few minutes to honestly answer the following questions:

- Have I been born by faith in Christ?
  —If so, briefly describe the circumstances related to your conversion.
  —If not, carefully reread the portion of this lesson that explains the basics of birth, and reconsider your need to be born-again.
- Have I passed the stage of spiritual infancy?
  —If so, give some reasons in support of your answer.
  —If not, consider some steps that will help you to continue growing in your faith.

Look . . . I'm Walking!

Romans 6:6–13, Ephesians 5:1–21

Learning how to walk is one of the most significant milestones in an infant's development. This is true not only physically but spiritually as well. If we want to grow into healthy Christian adults, we need to learn how to walk with God. And that involves living a Spirit-filled life—something many people talk about but few understand and even less seem to apply. What does it mean to walk with God in the power of the Spirit? How can such a lifestyle be lived? What are some of its benefits? We will seek to answer these questions as we turn to the Scriptures—our infallible guidebook on Christian growth.

I. Walking: An Understanding of Relevant Passages

When we turn to God's Word, we find several passages that express different aspects of the same action—*walking with God under the control of the Holy Spirit.* Let's survey some of these texts so that we can gain an understanding of this foundational activity of the Christian life.

A. Galatians 5:16. The Apostle Paul writes, "Walk by the Spirit, and you will not carry out the desire of the flesh." Living our lives God's way involves continual dependence on the Holy Spirit for guidance and power.

B. Colossians 1:9–10. In this passage Paul says that he has been praying unceasingly for the Colossian Christians "so that [they] may walk in a manner worthy of the Lord, to please Him in all respects, bearing fruit in every good work and increasing in the knowledge of God." The Greek term translated *worthy* means "of equal weight." When we walk in a way that honors God, our behavior meets His standard of holiness (cf. 1 Pet. 1:14–16).

C. 1 Thessalonians 2:10–12. In his letter to the believers at Thessalonica, Paul says,

> You are witnesses, and so is God, how devoutly and uprightly and blamelessly we behaved toward you believers; just as you know how we were exhorting and encouraging and imploring each one of you as a father would his own children, so that you may walk in a manner worthy of the God who calls you into His own kingdom and glory.

Paul and his co-workers diligently sought to model a mature Christian lifestyle before the Thessalonian believers and to motivate them toward godliness in all their conduct.

II. Walking: An Explanation of the Process

Now that we have a better idea of what it means to walk with God, we need to discover how this concept can be implemented in our lives. The dilemma, however, is that learning how to walk is not so much *taught* as it is *caught*. That is, there is no instruction manual that gives all the mechanics of living by the power of the Holy Spirit. The Bible does set forth some guiding principles, pertinent commands, and exemplary models regarding this spiritual activity. But the Word does not present a detailed plan for walking by the Spirit, because in many respects it varies from person to person. With this in mind, let's consider Ephesians 5:1–21. Here we will learn much of what the Bible teaches about this process.

A. Some essential commands. In verses 1–17, we are given several commands that need to be obeyed if we are to walk consistently with the Lord. First, we need to become "imitators of God"—those who conform themselves to God's character (v. 1; cf. Matt. 5:48, Luke 6:36). We can accomplish this by walking "in love, just as Christ also loved [us], and gave Himself up for us, an offering and a sacrifice to God as a fragrant aroma" (Eph. 5:2). Second, we are not to allow "immorality or any impurity or greed even [to] be named among [us]" (v. 3a). Third, we must replace "filthiness and silly talk, or coarse jesting" with thanksgiving for others (v. 4). Fourth, we are to grow in our discernment so that no one can deceive us "with empty words" (v. 6a). Fifth, we are exhorted not to engage in the darkened lifestyle of unbelievers but to "walk as children of light," producing fruit that "consists in all goodness and righteousness and truth" (vv. 7–9, 11a). Sixth, we need to be careful that we walk in wisdom, not foolishness, by using our time to please God (vv. 10, 15–16). And seventh, we are commanded to refrain from foolishness and to increase our understanding of God's will for His people concerning how they should conduct their lives (v. 17).

B. The central issue. How can all these commands be obeyed? The key is found in this verse: "Do not get drunk with wine, for that is dissipation, but be filled with the Spirit" (v. 18). The Greek word rendered *dissipation* literally means "incorrigible." In this context the term refers to a depraved and licentious lifestyle that is wasteful and controlled by wine. Rather than live this way, we are exhorted to "be filled with the Spirit" (v. 18b). This command does not refer to the indwelling ministry of the Holy Spirit. The Spirit's transforming work in an individual begins at the time of regeneration—the moment one is born into God's family (John 7:37–39, Rom. 8:9; 1 Cor. 2:12, 6:19–20; 1 John 4:13). However, the filling of the Spirit occurs as believers yield themselves to His control. Like the wind that effects a ship's movement when filling its sails, so the Holy Spirit influences our lives to help accomplish His perfect will in us. But in order for Him to do so, we must consciously submit to and cooperate with His character-changing activity each day. Romans 6 tells us how we can do this in three steps. First, we need to *know* "that our old self was crucified with [Christ], that our body of sin might be done away with, that we should no longer be slaves to sin; for he who has died is freed from sin" (Rom. 6:6–7). We who have accepted Christ as our Savior have been set free from sin. As a result, we no longer have to serve sin. We now have a new Master—Jesus Christ. Second, we need to *"consider* [ourselves] to be dead to sin, [and] alive to God in Christ Jesus" (v. 11, emphasis added). Since the power sin had over us was broken by Christ at our conversion, we are to reckon this as true by ceasing from committing sin (vv. 12–13a). And third, we need to *present* ourselves "to God as those alive from the dead, and [our] members as instruments of righteousness to God" (v. 13b). Moment by moment we should make ourselves available to God as His faithful servants. As we do, He will give us, through the power of His Spirit, all the resources we need to live a life that is both pleasing to Him and beneficial to us.

C. **Some practical benefits.** When we are filled with the Spirit, our lives begin to change. For example, our relationships with other people become deeper and more edifying (Eph. 5:19a). Our relationship to the Lord becomes more melodious and joyful (v. 19b). A spirit of gratitude begins to pervade our lives (v. 20), and an attitude of humility starts to characterize our associations with others (v. 21a). Our reverence of Christ also grows deeper when our lives are Spirit-filled (v. 21b).

III. Walking: It's Your Move

Living the Christian life is not highly complicated or deeply mysterious. Its basics are (1) realizing that we are free from sin's stranglehold, (2) living as if this were true, and (3) depending on God's Spirit to give us the supernatural power to live holy lives. Do you want to walk with God? His Spirit is available to help you, but it's up to you to take the first step.

Living Insights

Study One

Learning to walk is a normal part of growing up. It is a step-by-step motion that requires active involvement. This study centers around the source of strength that enables us to walk—the Spirit of God.

- It is vital to have a working knowledge of Romans 6 in order to understand walking by the Spirit. Let's break down the first fourteen verses into their simplest elements. Copy the following chart into your notebook, and look for *key words* throughout the passage. Using the text and a good Bible dictionary, *define* the words, and write down the *significance* each word has to walking in the Spirit. Two Bible dictionaries that you may find helpful are *Unger's Bible Dictionary,* by Merrill F. Unger, 3d ed. (Chicago: Moody Press, 1966), and *The Zondervan Pictorial Bible Dictionary,* 3d ed. (Grand Rapids: Regency Reference Library, Zondervan Publishing House, 1967).

Romans 6:1–14			
Key Words	Verses	Definitions	Significance

Living Insights

Study Two

The concept of walking by the Spirit is crucial to a vital Christian faith. Do you understand what it means to be Spirit-filled? Are you applying the Spirit's power to your life? Could you explain to someone else how he or she could submit to the Spirit's transforming work?

- Imagine that you have led someone to Jesus Christ through corresponding by mail. Now you are faced with the task of encouraging and discipling this person by the same means. Try writing this new believer a letter that explains what it means to walk by the Spirit. Remember, this person is young in the Lord, so use terms and illustrations that are easy to understand. Feel free to refer to the Scriptures often. After all, they are the nourishment spiritual newborns need most.

The Delights and Dangers of Childhood

Selected Scripture

One cannot become proficient in algebra, geometry, trigonometry, and calculus until one has mastered the basics of mathematics: addition, subtraction, multiplication, and division. There are no shortcuts. This is also true in the realm of Christian growth. Believers cannot become spiritually healthy adults until they pass through spiritual childhood, where they learn basic truths and acquire critical skills. This stage in the growth process can be delightful and rewarding. However, it can also be dangerous. If young Christians are spiritually abused, their spiritual growth can be stunted—sometimes permanently. It is important, therefore, for us to have a clear understanding of this essential stage of Christian growth. In this lesson we will zero in on spiritual childhood and discover some truths that can benefit us all.

I. The Growth Cycle: A Brief Review

As we have already seen, Christian growth cannot start until there has been spiritual birth. The infancy stage immediately follows conversion. During this period, Christians need a great deal of patience, attention, and instruction in order to survive. As spiritual infants learn how to pray, obey God, receive nourishment from His Word, and live the Spirit-filled life, they move into the stage of childhood. What they have learned as baby believers makes them increasingly curious about their faith. So they begin to ask more questions and personally probe their faith more deeply. As time passes, they grow into spiritual adolescence—a period marked by a prove-it-to-me attitude and topsy-turvy emotions. Adolescent believers strive to find their unique identity and purpose in Christ. In doing so, they begin reaching out for the responsibilities of adulthood while periodically retreating to the securities of childhood. In time, the confused stage of adolescence gives way to the ordered world of the adult. Here, self-confidence is gained, obedience to God is practiced, and service to others is given the importance it deserves. All Christians should strive for spiritual adulthood (Heb. 5:12–6:2). It is the period in which they can walk in the power of God's Spirit, feed themselves on God's Word, talk with the Lord regularly, and obey Him habitually. But this stage cannot be reached without first passing through the preceding stages of spiritual growth.

II. An Analysis of Spiritual Childhood: A Biblical Survey

As we focus on some of the biblical passages concerning spiritual childhood, we find that their teaching can be grouped into three categories—general observations, delightful strengths, and dangerous weaknesses. We will delve into the first two divisions here and examine the third in the next lesson.

A. General observations. God's Word makes several significant observations about childhood that are directly relevant to the spiritual realm. Let's consider three of them.

1. **Children have distinctive traits.** In the midst of the Apostle Paul's teaching on love is a verse that tells us a good deal about children. The verb tense Paul uses to communicate his point conveys continuous action in the past. Notice what he says: "When I was a child, I used to [continually] speak as a child, [continually] think as a child, [continually] reason as a child; when I became a man, I did away with childish things" (1 Cor. 13:11). Children speak, think, and reason differently than adults do. But as they grow in physical maturity, they are rightly expected to develop linguistically, mentally, and emotionally. However, serious problems can arise when people try to rush preteens into adulthood by demanding that they deny their natures and act older than they are. Among other things, this expectation places undue stress on children and often inhibits their desire and ability to grow into adulthood. This is also true in the spiritual world. Young Christians must be given the opportunity to be children so that they can mature into healthy spiritual adults.
2. **Children need parental accommodation.** To the new Christians at Corinth, Paul writes, "Here for this third time I am ready to come to you, and I will not be a burden to you; for I do not seek what is yours, but you; for children are not responsible to save up for their parents, but parents for their children" (2 Cor. 12:14). Paul had founded and established the Corinthian church (Acts 18:1–18). He was the Corinthian believers' spiritual parent, and consequently, desired that their growth in Christ be healthy. In order to accomplish this, he returned to them and cared for their needs without seeking any remuneration (2 Cor. 11:7–9; cf. 1 Cor. 9:18). The principle Paul seems to be acting on is this: Mature Christians should adapt themselves to the distinctive needs of immature believers in order to help ensure their healthy growth toward adulthood. For example, adult Christians should help spiritual children develop a sense of acceptance and identity. They also need to provide a context of security for young believers that promotes self-esteem. In addition, mature Christians can help immature saints establish a strong moral base by providing clear

channels of non-threatening communication. In short, children need protection from a world that threatens to demean and debase them by pushing them into adulthood before they are ready to handle it. Adult believers need to provide the opportunity for young Christians to be children while they are learning the lessons that will prepare them for greater maturity.

3. **Children require firm discipline.** The Bible is clear that children are not to be allowed to do whatever they please. Each child should be trained in a way that fits his or her unique personality and temperament. As Proverbs 22:6 states, "Train up a child in the way he should go [literally, according to his way], / Even when he is old he will not depart from it." This kind of upbringing requires the exercise of the type of discipline that will promote wisdom (v. 15, 23:13–14, 29:15). Again, this counsel applies not only to the physical arena but to the spiritual one as well. Sometimes Christians need to be corrected for both their own good and the welfare of the Body of Christ (cf. 1 Cor. 5:1–13, 2 Cor. 12:19–13:10, Heb. 12:5–13).[1]

B. Delightful strengths. Besides these general observations, the Bible presents numerous strengths that children possess. Let's look at some of them.

1. **Children are teachable and available.** Jesus made this point when He said, " 'Permit the children to come to Me; do not hinder them; for the kingdom of God belongs to such as these. Truly I say to you, whoever does not receive the kingdom of God like a child shall not enter it at all' " (Mark 10:14b–15). After speaking these words, He took the children "in His arms and began blessing them, laying His hands upon them" (v. 16). The Master enjoyed the presence of children, and they were receptive to His love.
2. **Children are trusting.** Youngsters implicitly trust those who are older than they. As such, they are at the mercy of the adults around them. The Lord understood and honored this when He requested that the children be allowed into His presence so that He could spend time with them.
3. **Children are spiritually ready to learn the Scriptures.** The Apostle Paul told Timothy, "Continue in the things you

1. Three books that accurately explain and illustrate the biblical teaching on church discipline are these: *Beyond Forgiveness: The Healing Touch of Church Discipline,* by Don Baker (Portland: Multnomah Press, 1984); *Healing the Wounded: The Costly Love of Church Discipline,* by John White and Ken Blue, foreword by Ray C. Stedman (Downers Grove: InterVarsity Press, 1985); *Restoring Fellowship,* by Joy P. Gage and Kenneth G. Gage (Chicago: Moody Press, 1984).

have learned and become convinced of, knowing from whom you have learned them; and that from childhood you have known the sacred writings which are able to give you the wisdom that leads to salvation through faith which is in Christ Jesus" (2 Tim. 3:14–15). The vast majority of people who become Christians do so between the ages of four and fourteen years old. This indicates that some of the best time for spiritual birth and growth is during the childhood years.

III. A Personal Evaluation: Some Relevant Questions

If you are a young believer, you are in one of the most exciting stages of your Christian life. Don't let others rob you of the joys of this time. Seek out individuals who will provide the environment and counsel you need for proper growth. If you are beyond the childhood stage of spiritual development, the healthy growth of other believers may depend on the way you respond to this lesson. Are you giving young believers the room to be children, or are you rushing them into adulthood? Are you adapting to their situation so as to meet their needs? Are you providing them with firm and loving supervision when necessary? Are you listening to them and taking their questions seriously? Are you praying for their spiritual welfare? Are you giving them a model worth emulating?

Living Insights

Study One

A well-known portion of Scripture dealing with children is found in Mark's Gospel. For many of us, it is a familiar scene that elicits pleasant feelings.

- Mark 10:13–16 records the scene where Christ takes the children in His arms and blesses them. Read this passage in the context of the entire tenth chapter. You may find it helpful to read it in a version of the Scriptures that you don't normally use. Reading this well-known passage in a different translation or paraphrase will bring a freshness to the text that you'll appreciate.

Living Insights

Study Two

Kids sure are fun to watch! Ask any parent. Or better yet, ask any grandparent! We can learn so much about ourselves through our children.

- Make a copy of the following chart in your notebook. Then, find an opportunity to observe some kids. Take about thirty minutes just to watch them relate to each other. As you jot down your observations, write down anything they do that reminds you of aspects of the spiritual life. Look especially for things that remind you of yourself at the childhood stage of spiritual growth.

The Delights of Childhood	
Observations	Spiritual Applications

Adult Talk about "Childish Things"

Selected Scripture

> When it comes to rearing children, every society is only 20 years away from barbarism. Twenty years is all we have to accomplish the task of civilizing the infants who are born into our midst each year. These savages know nothing of our language, our culture, our religion, our values, our customs of interpersonal relations. . . . *The barbarian must be tamed if civilization is to survive.*[1]

Dr. Albert Siegel is right—parents do have the important task of civilizing their children. Similarly, a critical part of a church's ministry is the evangelization of spiritual primitives and the development of their maturity in Christ. The fulfillment of these tasks is not essential for the survival of the universal Church. Christ made it clear that not even the powers of hell could destroy His Church (Matt. 16:18). However, local assemblies and individual believers will not become Christlike and reap the benefits of Christian maturity as long as they remain spiritually uncivilized. In order to become godly adults, believers need to grow out of spiritual childhood and put away "childish things" (1 Cor. 13:11). What are these childish things? How can we rid our lives of them? Let's see what Scripture has to say.

I. The Delightful Part: Childlikeness

Before we zero in on those characteristics of childhood that need to be put aside, let's highlight some childhood traits that should be encouraged.

A. Teachableness. Childlike Christians are often anxious to learn about their faith and ready to start exploring its many facets. We should never outgrow this insatiable desire to learn about God and the application of His truth.

B. Touchableness. Like children, young believers are generally willing to let down their guard, place their trust in others, and become involved in people's lives. This level of transparency and vulnerability should always characterize a Christian's life.

C. Tenderness. Christians who are childlike in their faith are usually open to God's Word and respond positively to the Spirit's work in their lives. The Lord desires that all His people manifest this sensitivity to Him.

II. The Difficult Part: Childishness

Unfortunately, there are some aspects of spiritual childhood that are hindrances to Christian growth. These negative traits need to be

1. Dr. Albert Siegel as quoted by Gordon MacDonald, *The Effective Father* (Wheaton: Tyndale House Publishers, 1977), p. 94.

brought under control—tamed, if you will. The Bible reveals at least four of them.

A. Willful defiance. Childish Christians often rebel against authority. They do not want to hear or accept anything that places uncomfortable demands on them. Rather than live by God's standard, they follow their own desires. During the prophet Isaiah's ministry, many of the Israelites acted this way. The Lord described their childish behavior with words of condemnation:

> "Woe to the rebellious children," declares the Lord,
> "Who execute a plan, but not Mine,
> And make an alliance, but not of My Spirit,
> In order to add sin to sin;
> Who proceed down to Egypt,
> Without consulting Me." (Isa. 30:1–2a)

The Lord spoke similarly of the Israelites through the prophet Jeremiah. In piercing terms, God exposed the reason for and result of the Jews' defiance:

> "My people are foolish,
> They know Me not;
> They are stupid children,
> And they have no understanding.
> They are shrewd to do evil,
> But to do good they do not know." (Jer. 4:22)
> " 'Hear this, O foolish and senseless people,
> Who have eyes, but see not;
> Who have ears, but hear not.
> Do you not fear Me?' declares the Lord.
> 'Do you not tremble in My presence?...
> But this people has a stubborn and rebellious heart;
> They have turned aside and departed.
> They do not say in their heart,
> "Let us now fear the Lord our God" ' "
> (5:21–22a, 23–24a).

As God's children, we must learn to yield our wills to Him. Our submission will not only honor the Lord, but it will allow us to reap the blessings that He longs to give us.

B. Superficial commitment. Childish believers often desire to be entertained instead of transformed. They enjoy listening to great preachers and beautiful music. They may even serve in the church from time to time, but they have no genuine interest in heeding the truth on a practical level. God warned the prophet Ezekiel about such people. Notice what He said:

> "As for you, [Ezekiel], your countrymen are talking together about you by the walls and at the doors of

> the houses, saying to each other, 'Come and hear the message that has come from the Lord.' My people come to you, as they usually do, and sit before you to listen to your words, but they do not put them into practice. With their mouths they express devotion, but their hearts are greedy for unjust gain. Indeed, to them you are nothing more than one who sings love songs with a beautiful voice and plays an instrument well, for they hear your words but do not put them into practice."[2] (Ezek. 33:30–32)

The Lord is not pleased with superficial commitments. He wants our hearts and wills, not just our words and thoughts. If we desire to become spiritual adults, we need to put our faith into action. As the Apostle James states, we must "prove [ourselves] doers of the word, and not merely hearers who delude themselves" (James 1:22).

C. Overly impressed. Another characteristic of spiritual childishness is a misplaced emphasis on people. Rather than give their ultimate allegiance to the Savior, childish believers often unduly commit themselves to His servants. This problem arose in the early days of the Corinthian church. The local assembly experienced disunity and dissension because many of its members were quarrelling over who followed the greatest leader. Some were proud that they listened only to Paul. Others held up Apollos or Cephas as their authorities. Apparently, some believers even refused to submit to any human leader because they were devoted only to Christ (1 Cor. 1:11–12). In the first part of his letter, the Apostle Paul challenged these childish attitudes and practices with a series of rhetorical questions: "Has Christ been divided? Paul was not crucified for you, was he? Or were you baptized in the name of Paul?" (v. 13). Later in the same letter, Paul addressed the issue again even more directly:

> You are still fleshly. For since there is jealousy and strife among you, are you not fleshly, and are you not walking like mere men? For when one says, "I am of Paul," and another, "I am of Apollos," are you not mere men? What then is Apollos? And what is Paul? Servants through whom you believed, even as the Lord gave opportunity to each one. I planted, Apollos watered, but God was causing the growth. So then neither the one who plants nor the one who waters is anything, but God who causes the growth. . . . So then let no one boast in men. (3:3–7, 21a)

2. *The NIV Study Bible* (Grand Rapids: Zondervan Bible Publishers, 1985).

It is true that God uses certain individuals to significantly impact our lives for Christ. And we should express our gratitude to them for being faithful servants of the Lord. However, we should never exalt them to a godlike status, for that is idolatry—a sin we are exhorted to guard ourselves against (1 John 5:21).

Dangers of Idolatry

When one's devotion to something is greater than it is to God, one has become an idolater. Idol worship consists of making an ultimate commitment to that which is less than ultimate. There are at least four dangers inherent in this sin. First, *idolatry stagnates our knowledge*. It causes us to become closed-minded toward the truth and defensive about our failure to practice it. Second, *idolatry steals our allegiance*. Our loyalty to God begins to wane as our allegiance to others deepens. Third, *idolatry strains our balance*. Since people and things cannot always deliver what they promise, excessive devotion to them will eventually disillusion us and send us into a spiritual tailspin. And fourth, *idolatry stunts our growth*. We will never grow in Christ as long as our ultimate allegiance is placed elsewhere. We need to get our eyes off people and things and "[fix] our eyes on Jesus, the author and perfecter of faith" (Heb. 12:2a).

D. Easily swayed. In Ephesians 4, Paul mentions another mark of spiritual childishness. After explaining that the goal of Christian ministry is to help all believers become spiritual adults (vv. 11–13), he specifies a trait of immaturity that blocks this growth: "We are no longer to be children, tossed here and there by waves, and carried about by every wind of doctrine, by the trickery of men, by craftiness in deceitful scheming" (v. 14). The Greek word translated *trickery* means "wicked dice-playing," and it speaks of intentional fraud.[3] The phrase "craftiness in deceitful scheming" refers to unscrupulous behavior designed to lead people away from the path of truth. Paul is saying that childish Christians are easily swayed by the latest fashion in religious thinking. Consequently, they are frequently lured away from the Christian faith. The only way immature believers can avoid spiritual seduction is to commit themselves to continual growth in Christ.

3. Fritz Reinecker, *A Linguistic Key to the Greek New Testament*, edited by Cleon L. Rogers, Jr. (Grand Rapids: Zondervan Publishing House, 1980), p. 532.

III. The Desirable Part: Getting Rid of "Childish Things"

How can we remain childlike while putting away childish things? How can we become spiritually civilized? We can lay aside the negatives of spiritual childhood by implementing three thoughts into our lives.

A. We dare not remain childish. Willful defiance, superficial commitment, overly impressionable minds, and easily swayed wills must be recognized as barriers to spiritual maturity. We need to be aware of their destructive potential and seek God's strength to overcome them.

B. We must not ignore our responsibility. The Lord has given us the Holy Spirit to transform our lives into Christ-likeness. However, it is our responsibility to cooperate with the Spirit's work in our lives by seeking to obey God's Word.

C. We cannot escape the tension between our nature and our need. We all are born into the world with rebellious natures (Ps. 51:5, Eph. 2:3). And we willingly give in to our evil inclinations, even after we have accepted Christ by faith (James 1:13–15). This creates a real tension in our lives. Although we still want to go our own way, we have a need to conform our lives to His righteous standard. The only way we can ease this tension is to submit regularly to Christ's authority as we obey His Word by the power of His Spirit.

Living Insights

Study One

One of the first references we looked at in this lesson was Isaiah 30. Let's take some time to uncover the riches embedded in this chapter.

- Read Isaiah 30:1–33. Then read it again more carefully, using a copy of the following chart to help sort out your thoughts. Zero in on both the childish and the godly traits mentioned in the passage. You should find a good amount of each.

Childishness and Godliness—Isaiah 30:1–33			
Childish Behavior	Verses	Godly Behavior	Verses

Living Insights

Study Two

Let's continue this adult talk about "childish things" by gathering a group of adults together for a discussion. Use the following suggestions as guidelines for your time together. Encourage everyone to participate by providing an atmosphere of acceptance and understanding.

—How do adults show childlike intellectual teachability . . . emotional touchability . . . spiritual tenderness?

—How do adults show childish willful defiance . . . superficial commitment . . . idolatrous allegiance . . . tendencies to be spiritually seduced?

Three Proofs of Growth

Matthew 10:1–10, Acts 4:32–37

One of the most remarkable eras in Church history took place during the first century. Shortly after Christ had ascended into heaven, His disciples began leading infant believers to exciting vistas of faith. It was not long before many of these new Christians began to show evidence of maturity. What principles did they apply that helped them grow? How were those principles worked out in their lives? What do Christians today need to do in order to experience the same growth the early believers did? In this lesson we will examine two passages of Scripture that will help us answer these questions. Let's remain open to the counsel they give.

I. Discovering Three Principles from Jesus' Teaching

During the first several months of Christ's earthly ministry, the twelve disciples spent most of their time watching the Master work and listening to His words. Eventually, however, a time came when the Twelve needed to put the truth they were learning into action. Matthew 10:1–10 records their initiation into Christian service. In this passage, we find three principles that guided their actions and aided their spiritual growth.

A. Unity. The text informs us that Jesus called the Twelve together and gave them instructions for service (Matt. 10:1–4a). Mark 6:7 adds that Jesus even "[sent] them out in pairs." The Lord never intended that His followers live out their faith alone. Instead, He encourages His people to work together. The principle displayed by His actions with the Twelve is this: *There is strength in staying close together.* Ecclesiastes 4:9–13 amplifies this truth. There we learn that going through life with a companion is better than living life alone. Why? Because two "have a good return for their labor" (v. 9). Also, "if either of them falls, the one will lift up his companion. . . . Furthermore, if two lie down together they keep warm, but how can one be warm alone? And if one can overpower him who is alone, two can resist him" (vv. 10–12a). Not only does unity bring strength, it encourages spiritual growth. Christ indicated as much when He prayed to His Father in behalf of all Christians. Consider His words:

> "And for their sakes I sanctify Myself, that they themselves also may be *sanctified in truth.* I do not ask in behalf of these alone, but for those also who believe in Me through their word; that they may all be one; even as Thou, Father, art in Me, and I in Thee, that they also may be in Us; that the world may believe that Thou didst send Me. And the glory which

Thou hast given Me I have given to them; that they may be one, just as We are one; I in them, and Thou in Me, that they may be *perfected in unity*, that the world may know that Thou didst send Me, and didst love them, even as Thou didst love Me." (John 17:19–23, emphasis added)

B. Authority. Looking back to Matthew 10, we see that Jesus gave the twelve disciples "authority over unclean spirits, to cast them out, and to heal every kind of disease and every kind of sickness" (v. 1b; cf. vv. 7–8a). In other words, Jesus acknowledged that *there is power in doing God's work.* This power comes not from any human resource but from the sovereign hand of God. The Apostle Paul revealed this truth about his own ministry when he penned these statements to the believers at Corinth:

> And when I came to you, brethren, I did not come with superiority of speech or of wisdom, proclaiming to you the testimony of God. For I determined to know nothing among you except Jesus Christ, and Him crucified. And I was with you in weakness and in fear and in much trembling. And my message and my preaching were not in persuasive words of wisdom, but in demonstration of the Spirit and of power, that your faith should not rest on the wisdom of men, but on the power of God. (1 Cor. 2:1–5)

Believers who do God's work dependent on His Spirit have the authority of heaven at their disposal. Realizing this fact gives them confidence before people and humility before God, both of which are marks of spiritual maturity.

C. Generosity. Before Jesus sent the Twelve on their way, He told them, " 'Freely you received, freely give. Do not acquire gold, or silver, or copper for your money belts, or a bag for your journey, or even two tunics, or sandals, or a staff; for the worker is worthy of his support' " (Matt. 10:8b–10). Christ wanted the disciples to discover that *there is freedom in giving without restraint.* Jesus had not exacted a fee from the Twelve for the instruction He had given them. Therefore, He did not want the disciples to charge others for their service. He expected that their needs would be met willingly by those who would benefit from their ministry. This approach gave the disciples freedom to serve beyond what others expected of them.

II. Modeling These Principles in the Early Church

According to Acts 4:32–37, the disciples learned the principles of unity, authority, and generosity well, and passed them on to the early Church. These verses give us an inside look at how the spiritual newborns in Jerusalem were growing up.

A. Unity in action. We read that "the congregation of those who believed were of one heart and soul; and not one of them claimed that anything belonging to him was his own; but all things were common property to them" (v. 32). These new Christians were committed to the welfare and growth of one another. Those who had the resources to meet the needs of others willingly did so. This practice was not a form of communism—the involuntary even distribution of wealth—but a free expression of sacrificial love to those in need. These young believers practiced what the Apostle Paul exhorted the Philippian Christians to do: "Make my joy complete by being of the same mind, maintaining the same love, united in spirit, intent on one purpose. Do nothing from selfishness or empty conceit, but with humility of mind let each of you regard one another as more important than himself" (Phil. 2:2–3).

B. Authority on display. In Acts 4, we are also told that "with great power the apostles were giving witness to the resurrection of the Lord Jesus, and abundant grace was upon them all" (v. 33). The Lord blessed the early Church's growth and ministry as the apostles proclaimed the good news about Christ. The Jerusalem Christians were clearly more concerned with furthering God's kingdom than promoting their local assemblies. The difference in emphasis is critical, as Howard A. Snyder explains:

> The church gets in trouble whenever it thinks it is in the church business rather than the Kingdom business.
>
> In the church business, people are concerned with church activities, religious behavior and spiritual things. In the Kingdom business, people are concerned with Kingdom activities, all human behavior and everything God has made, visible and invisible. Kingdom people see human affairs as saturated with spiritual meaning and Kingdom significance.
>
> Kingdom people seek first the Kingdom of God and its justice; church people often put church work above concerns of justice, mercy and truth. Church people think about how to get people into the church; Kingdom people think about how to get the church into the world. Church people worry that the world might change the church; Kingdom people work to see the church change the world. . . .
>
> If the church has one great need, it is this: To be set free for the Kingdom of God, to be liberated from

itself as it has become in order to be itself as God intends.[1]

C. Generosity exemplified. The early Christians also shared sacrificially with one another. Notice what Acts 4 records:

> There was not a needy person among them, for all who were owners of land or houses would sell them and bring the proceeds of the sales, and lay them at the apostles' feet; and they would be distributed to each, as any had need. And Joseph, a Levite of Cyprian birth, who was also called Barnabas by the apostles (which translated means, Son of Encouragement), and who owned a tract of land, sold it and brought the money and laid it at the apostles' feet. (vv. 34–37)

They did not hoard their belongings but offered them to meet the needs of other believers.

III. Putting These Principles into Practice Today

The Lord's desire for His children has not changed since the first century. He still wants them to strive for unity, serve with authority, and give with generosity. How can we who are Christians do these things? The answer is threefold.

A. We must maintain closeness in order to experience unity.

B. We must remember who is Lord in order to minister with authority.

C. We must hold our possessions loosely in order to practice generosity.

Living Insights

Study One

In this lesson we have looked at three proofs of growth—*unity, authority,* and *generosity.* Are these evidences of growth woven through the entire New Testament? Let's do some investigating.

- Make a copy of the following chart in your notebook. Using your Bible and a concordance, look up the words in the chart below, and list the references cited from the New Testament. Then write a summary of what each passage is stating.

Continued on next page

1. Howard A. Snyder, *Liberating the Church: The Ecology of Church and Kingdom* (Downers Grove: InterVarsity Press, 1982), p. i.

Three Proofs of Growth		
Words	References	Summaries
Unity, One		
Authority, Power		
Gave, Give, Giving		

Living Insights

Study Two

Most of us can probably remember the growth charts we made when we were kids. They may have been placed on the back of a closet door, on a wall in the kitchen, or anywhere else that was convenient. Let's use the same technique for measuring spiritual growth.

- On the first chart give yourself a numerical measurement for your commitment to *unity and accountability.* On the second one rate your commitment to *authority and obedience,* and on the third indicate your level of commitment to *generosity and unselfishness.* Then, take some time to reflect on your ratings and how you can improve them.

Unity and Accountability	Authority and Obedience	Generosity and Unselfishness
10	10	10
9	9	9
8	8	8
7	7	7
6	6	6
5	5	5
4	4	4
3	3	3
2	2	2
1	1	1

Adolescents in Adult Bodies

Selected Scripture

Most of us probably remember the story of Peter Pan—a boy who refused to grow up. Wishing to escape the responsibilities of adulthood, Peter Pan was determined to stay eternally young and carefree in Never Never Land. There is something attractive about this playful approach to life. It offers us the joys of childhood and adolescence without the responsibilities of adulthood. And those who embrace this idealistic lifestyle become like Peter Pan—a youngster "caught in the abyss between the man he didn't want to become and the boy he could no longer be."[1] As Dan Kiley explains, the consequences of the Peter Pan syndrome can be tragic:

> Children who follow in the footsteps of Peter Pan eventually experience a serious psychological problem that usually leads to social maladjustment. Many of them are emotionally crippled and interpersonally inept. Feelings of isolation and failure abound as they encounter a society that has little patience with adults who act like children. But these people see no reason why they should feel so bad. Viewing their problem as temporary, they do their best to forget about it. Needless to say, it gets worse.[2]

Spiritually speaking, there are many people who become children of God but never become adults. Although they may be in their twenties or older, they remain spiritual teenagers. The Bible gives us several examples of Christian adolescents wrapped in adult bodies. We will consider three of these figures in order to better discern our stage of spiritual growth and learn how we can guard ourselves against permanent adolescence.

I. Undeniable Characteristics of Adolescent Adults

There are at least three traits that identify adolescent adults.

A. Instability when the going is rough. Teenage-like adults do not have staying power during difficult times. When the road they are traveling becomes rugged, they veer off and seek out a less demanding path. And if the new way becomes unpleasant, still another road is sought. In short, adolescent adults are too unstable to be obedient "over a long period of time and in a single direction."[3]

1. Dan Kiley, *The Peter Pan Syndrome: Men Who Have Never Grown Up* (New York: Dodd, Mead and Co., 1983), p. 23.

2. Kiley, *Peter Pan Syndrome,* p. 25.

3. Friedrich Nietzsche, *Beyond Good and Evil,* translated by Walter Kaufmann (New York: Vintage Books, 1966), sec. 188, p. 101. Eugene Peterson develops Nietzsche's observation from a biblical perspective in his book *A Long Obedience in the Same Direction: Discipleship in an Instant Society* (Downers Grove: InterVarsity Press, 1980).

B. Irresponsibility when the world is appealing. Adolescent adults can frequently resist mild allurements. But when faced with greater temptations to sin, they often succumb without much of a fight.

C. Insensitivity when the will is challenged. Immature adults are usually stubborn. They refuse to listen to the advice of others, and they are unwilling to give up their rights for the good of those around them.

II. First-Century Examples of Adolescent Adults

The adolescent characteristics of instability, irresponsibility, and insensitivity are exemplified by three New Testament believers—John Mark, Demas, and Diotrephes. Let's consider what the Bible says about the spiritual immaturity of these men.

A. John Mark: A man who walked away. Prior to Paul's first missionary journey, Barnabas and Paul left Jerusalem and went to Antioch, taking with them a young Christian named John Mark (Acts 12:25–13:3). We can imagine that this must have been quite an honor for John Mark. After all, he was traveling with two of the most well known and highly respected Christians of his day. He probably thought about all that he could learn from his companions and perhaps even dreamt that he would be part of the evangelization of all the known world. John Mark's idealism must have flourished when he sailed with Paul and Barnabas to the port of Salamis, a beautiful city that had a large Jewish population.[4] Amidst the magnificent sights of this city, he helped Paul and Barnabas "proclaim the word of God" (13:5). This positive experience may have caused John Mark to think that missionary work would always be pleasant and involve little struggle. However, he would soon learn that this was not the case. From Salamis the three missionaries traveled to Paphos, where they encountered a hostile magician named Elymas (v. 8). John Mark witnessed Paul's confrontation with Elymas and saw how "a mist and a darkness fell upon [Elymas]," causing him to seek "those who would lead him by the hand" (v. 11b). This encounter must have dealt quite a blow to John Mark's idealistic perspective of missionary work. Eventually, Paul, Barnabas, and John Mark left Paphos and sailed to "Perga in Pamphylia"—a rugged, mountainous coastal region in Asia Minor (v. 13a). Sometime after their arrival, "John [Mark] left them and returned to Jerusalem" (v. 13b). The Bible does not tell us why John Mark went home. However, "there is some

4. More information on Salamis can be found in these sources: *Archaeology in Bible Lands,* by Howard F. Vos (Chicago: Moody Press, 1977), pp. 302–3; "Salamis," by W. Harold Mare, in *The New International Dictionary of Biblical Archaeology* (Grand Rapids: Regency Reference Library, Zondervan Publishing House, 1983), pp. 393–94.

evidence Paul became quite ill in Perga, possibly with malaria, as the city of Perga was subject to malarial infections. Furthermore, Paul preached to the people of Galatia 'because of an illness' (Gal. 4:13). The missionary party may have gone inland to higher ground to avoid the ravages of malaria."[5] These events may have resulted in a loss of courage, confidence, and optimism on John Mark's part, causing him to abandon his companions. Whatever the cause, we do know that Paul was greatly upset by John Mark's defection. We can see this in his refusal to take John Mark on a second missionary journey (Acts 15:36–40). At this point in his life, John Mark was too unstable to handle the rigors and perils of missionary life. When the going got rough, he quit, revealing his adolescent spiritual state.

Personal Application

How do you handle difficult situations? Do you run away from them, or do you stand and face them? Spiritual adults do not quit when the road becomes rough.

B. Demas: A man who loved the world. We know from Colossians 4:14 and Philemon 23–24 that Demas was a Christian and a co-worker of Luke and Paul. However, we learn in 2 Timothy that while Paul was imprisoned in Rome, Demas deserted him (4:10; cf. 1:8, 16–17). He abandoned Paul because he "loved this present world" (4:10a). Rather than keep his attention on Christ and heavenly rewards (v. 8), Demas succumbed to the lure of comfort and earthly treasures.

Personal Application

Are you being drawn away from Christ by temporary pleasures? Are you more earthly-minded than heavenly-minded? Spiritual adults realize that the joys of sin are fleeting, while the benefits of holiness last forever (Matt. 6:19–21, 2 Tim. 4:7–8).

C. Diotrephes: A man who wanted his way. In 3 John we read of an individual who was a self-appointed leader in his church. He wanted to be in charge and have everyone follow his counsel only. The Apostle John wrote this about him:

> I wrote something to the church; but Diotrephes, who loves to be first among them, does not accept what we say. For this reason, if I come, I will call attention

5. Stanley D. Toussaint, "Acts," in *The Bible Knowledge Commentary: New Testament Edition*, edited by John F. Walvoord and Roy B. Zuck (Wheaton: Victor Books, 1983), pp. 388–89.

to his deeds which he does, unjustly accusing us with wicked words; and not satisfied with this, neither does he himself receive the brethren, and he forbids those who desire to do so, and puts them out of the church. Beloved, do not imitate what is evil, but what is good. The one who does good is of God; the one who does evil has not seen God. (3 John 9–11)

> ***Personal Application***
>
> Are you a self-appointed leader and critic? Do you lack respectful love and point an accusing finger at others without adequate warrant? Are you open to the counsel of others, even if it exposes weaknesses in your character and walk with God? Spiritual adults are not prideful and defensive, but humble and vulnerable.

III. Ways to Guard against Permanent Spiritual Adolescence

All Christians must pass through spiritual adolescence, but no believer has to *remain* at this stage of growth. We can guard ourselves against the Peter Pan syndrome by making three principles a practical part of our lives.

A. When wrestling with restlessness, realize the benefits of faithfulness.

B. When lured by irresponsibility, think of the consequences of carnality.

C. When tempted to manipulate and dominate, remember the lordship of Christ.

Living Insights

Study One

Spiritual adolescents commonly possess three character traits—*instability, irresponsibility,* and *insensitivity.* Let's turn our attention to an Old Testament judge who demonstrated these traits.

- Copy the chart from the following page into your notebook, then turn to Judges 14–16. As you read Samson's story, jot down incidents that relate to the three characteristics of adolescence mentioned above. This should prove to be an insightful study of a man who never fully grew up.

Samson: An Adolescent in an Adult Body		
Marks of Instability	Marks of Irresponsibility	Marks of Insensitivity

Living Insights

Study Two

Here are some questions worth thinking about: How was your adolescence? What were some of the good things about those years? What problems were especially prevalent during that period? What did you learn as a result of your teenage years? Take some time to record your thoughts on a page in your journal.

Remembering My Adolescence

When Peter Pan Comes to Church

1 Corinthians

Since God *is* truth, all truth is His truth (Ps. 31:5b; John 1:14, 14:6; 1 John 5:7). And because He wants His people to be like Him, the Lord commands them to learn the truth and apply it to their lives (Josh. 1:7–8, 24:14; John 4:24; 2 Cor. 4:2; Eph. 4:25, 6:14). When believers do this, they develop *wisdom*—the ability to "discern good and evil" (Heb. 5:14b). And the more wisdom they gain, the more mature they become. We learned in the last lesson that adolescent adults often suffer from the Peter Pan syndrome. Rather than push forward to spiritual adulthood through the consistent application of divine truth, they choose to remain spiritual teenagers by refusing to fully submit to God's Word. We will see in this lesson that the consequences of this choice can be devastating to individuals and congregations alike.

I. The Peter Pan Syndrome: A Brief Review

As infant believers grow in their faith, they absorb new information at an amazing rate. By the time they reach spiritual adolescence, they usually have enough knowledge to move forward to adulthood, but they often lack the wisdom necessary to accurately apply the knowledge they have. This situation frequently produces personal frustration and insecurity as well as tensions with other believers. Fortunately, Christians can grow out of spiritual adolescence and greatly benefit from it if they persevere at growing up God's way. But if believers refuse to accept the responsibilities of godly adulthood, they will remain spiritual teenagers. Christians who take this path suffer from the Peter Pan syndrome. And they are not difficult to spot. Those who are afflicted with this malady exhibit such traits as irresponsibility, anxiety, loneliness, selfishness, unaccountability, instability, and procrastination. In short, their focus is self-centered, and their attitude is one of resistance, not cooperation.

II. A Biblical Example: The Corinthian Church

A local assembly that has Peter Pan Christians can suffer greatly as a result of the immaturity they perpetuate. An excellent illustration of this truth is the first-century church in Corinth. The city in which the Corinthian believers lived was well known for its idolatry and immorality, as well as its prosperity. In fact, a thousand female prostitutes served at the temple of Aphrodite—the goddess of love and beauty—which stood on top of the highest mountain just south of Corinth. "It is to this evil trade carried on in the name of religion that Strabo, the geographer, ascribed the prosperity of the city."[1] Corinth was so notorious for its immorality that the words

1. Donald H. Madvig, "Corinth," in *The International Standard Bible Encyclopedia*, 4 vols., rev. ed. (Grand Rapids: William B. Eerdmans Publishing Co., 1979, 1982), vol. 1, p. 773.

Corinthianize—meaning "to practice immorality"—and *Corinthian girl*—referring to a prostitute—were coined as early as the fourth century B.C.[2] Given this kind of environment, it is easy to see how spiritually young Christians could have difficulties growing up in their faith. In one of his letters to the Corinthian church, Paul addresses four problems the church was experiencing, each of which reveals a common characteristic of spiritual adolescence. The traits he unveils are great anxiety, personal immaturity, overt immorality, and unrestrained liberty. Let's examine each of them in more detail.

A. Great anxiety. The Corinthian assembly exhibited many telltale signs of extreme tension. For example, there were factions in the church that quarreled over which leader was the best to follow (1 Cor. 1:10–12, 3:3–4). This divisiveness brought about serious abuses in the assembly's observance of the Lord's Supper and in its exercise of spiritual gifts during the worship service (11:17–34, 14:22–23, 39–40). Strange as it may seem, this marvelously blessed church lacked unity (1:5–7). The same phenomenon occurs today. A congregation with spiritual adolescents usually experiences internal strife and jealousy. This tension is frequently produced because adolescent Christians (1) tend to expect too much from both themselves and other believers, (2) are often given to extremes in their thinking and behavior, and (3) usually deny personal responsibility for failures and find it difficult to forgive those who offend them. With Christians like this in local churches, it is little wonder that congregations have to work so hard at developing and maintaining a spirit of harmony.

B. Personal immaturity. The believers in Corinth were also immature. Paul said as much when he wrote, "I, brethren, could not speak to you as to spiritual men, but as to men of flesh, as to babes in Christ. I gave you milk to drink, not solid food; for you were not yet able to receive it. Indeed, even now you are not yet able, for you are still fleshly" (3:1–3a). Apparently, the Corinthian Christians had the information they needed for proper growth, but they were applying it either irresponsibly or not at all. Paul's desire was that they become responsible, trustworthy believers. And that involves at least seven things: self-discipline, respect for authority, being true to one's word, bearing one's share of the load, voluntary accountability, unselfish serving, and moral integrity. Unfortunately, adolescent congregations tend to downplay these traits rather than encourage their development.

2. Madvig, "Corinth," p. 773. For more information on Corinth see the book *Jesus and Paul: Places They Knew,* by F. F. Bruce (Nashville: Thomas Nelson Publishers, 1981), pp. 101–5.

C. Overt immorality. Another characteristic of spiritual adolescence displayed in the Corinthian church was unchallenged sexual immorality. Notice what Paul said: "It is actually reported that there is immorality among you, and immorality of such a kind as does not exist even among the Gentiles, that someone has his father's wife. And you have become arrogant, and have not mourned instead, in order that the one who had done this deed might be removed from your midst" (5:1–2). The Apostle was shocked that the assembly at Corinth had not disciplined the believer involved in incest. Paul exhorted the church to discipline this man by publicly removing him from their fellowship so that he could be restored to a right relationship with God (vv. 4–13; cf. 2 Cor. 2:6–8).[3] This was not the only instance of immorality in the church. Paul noted that some believers were sexually involved with prostitutes—perhaps the very ones who served at the temple of Aphrodite (1 Cor. 6:15–16). The Corinthian believers were commanded to "flee immorality" rather than engage in sexually promiscuous activities (v. 18a). The Greek term translated *immorality* in this verse refers to any kind of sexual sin. Therefore, the word encompasses adultery, incest, premarital sex, homosexuality, and bestiality. In short, any form of sexual intimacy shared outside of the marriage relationship is immoral. Consequently, Christians should strive for sexual purity in every relationship.

D. Unrestrained liberty. The spiritual adolescents in Corinth were also abusing their Christian freedom. Some historical background will help us understand what was involved. A common practice in Greek and Roman forms of idol worship was the burning of less desirable portions of an animal as a sacrifice and the retaining of choicer sections for personal consumption. The parts of the animal that were spared in the sacrifices were sold in meat markets, which were often located in or near pagan temples.[4] Apparently, many of the Corinthian Christians were frequenting these markets in order to buy meat for their tables (10:25). It also seems that at least some of these believers were participating in meals of celebration which were held in the temples following the pagan sacrifices (8:10). Paul did not think that these actions were inherently wrong. He realized that since idols are not real gods, to eat the meat of animals sacrificed to imaginary beings was inconsequential (vv. 1–6, 10:19–20a; cf. Ps. 115:4–8). "However," Paul writes, "not

3. See page 27, footnote 1, in this study guide for some helpful resources on church discipline.

4. David K. Lowery, "1 Corinthians," in *The Bible Knowledge Commentary: New Testament Edition,* edited by John F. Walvoord and Roy B. Zuck (Wheaton: Victor Books, 1983), p. 521.

all men have this knowledge; but some, being accustomed to the idol until now, eat food as if it were sacrificed to an idol [that is, a real god]; and their conscience being weak is defiled" (1 Cor. 8:7). Apparently, some of the Corinthian believers were not convinced "that an idol was nothing and that there was only one [true] God."[5] As a result, "they . . . had not come to the point where they could accept eating this kind of meat as a matter of indifference. For them it was wrong, and so to eat it was sin (cf. Rom. 14:23)."[6] Because of these weaker brethren, Paul exhorted the stronger believers to exercise their Christian liberty with love and discernment (1 Cor. 8:9–13, 10:23–33; cf. Rom. 14:13–21).

III. Some Practical Advice: A Personal Analysis

All Scripture has been given by the Lord so that His people can grow in the knowledge and application of the truth (2 Tim. 3:16–17). Given this, we need to take time to personally consider what we have studied in this lesson. Let's do that now by honestly answering four questions directed especially at spiritual adolescents.

A. What am I gaining by remaining immature?

B. Why am I refusing to model moral purity?

C. Who am I hurting through the misuse of my liberty?

D. When am I going to come to terms with my responsibility to grow up?

Living Insights

Study One

You don't have to look far in the Scriptures to find an example of an adolescent church. In Paul's first letter to the Corinthians, we read about just such a congregation.

- After copying the following chart, return to the four chapters in 1 Corinthians that we have discussed. As you read chapters 1, 3, 5, and 8, look for answers to the questions given in the chart. Try to discover the answers from the biblical text alone. This is one of the best methods of observation in Bible study.

Continued on next page

5. Lowery, "1 Corinthians," p. 521.
6. Lowery, "1 Corinthians," p. 521.

When Peter Pan Comes to Church—1 Corinthians 1, 3, 5, 8	
Questions	Answers
Who?	
What?	
Where?	
When?	
Why?	
How?	

Living Insights

Study Two

Even though nobody wants to think of themselves as spiritually adolescent, it's a stage we all must go through on our way to Christian maturity. Let's stop and think about how we can help fellow believers through this difficult stage.

—What can I do to encourage someone toward maturity?
—How can I become a better model of moral purity?
—Who can I help become more wise in the use of their liberty?
—When am I going to begin helping fellow Christians come to terms with growing up?

What's *Right* about Adolescence?

Selected Scripture

For the most part, our portrayal of spiritual adolescence has been grim. Lest we get the impression that this stage brings nothing but headaches, heartaches, pressure, and pain, we need to be reminded that adolescence is frequently characterized by remarkable growth and achievement. Indeed, some of the most exciting and challenging times of spiritual development can occur during this stage. The Bible supports this fact by providing us with a record of several adolescents who lived exemplary lives even when the odds were against them. In this lesson we will take a look at the positive side of spiritual youth as we focus on four of these godly young lives.

I. Some Positive Traits Found among Teenagers

Adolescents who are maturing spiritually manifest many strengths in their lives. Among these positive qualities, four are particularly common. One is a *willingness to risk.* This is the readiness to abandon what is secure and familiar in order to explore that which is new and challenging. Another is a *sensitivity to God.* Teenagers are frequently open to the Word and willing to apply its instruction. Still another strength is a *commitment to integrity*... the desire to live out one's convictions. The last is a *determination to stand.* Rather than buckle under pressure, many adolescents have the tenacity to remain firm in their walk with God.

II. Some Scriptural Examples of These Traits

Four teenagers from biblical times that illustrate these qualities are Isaac, Samuel, Josiah, and Daniel. Let's examine the scriptural record regarding these youths so that we can see what it means to be willing to risk, sensitive to God, committed to integrity, and determined to stand.

A. Isaac. When Abraham was one hundred years old and his wife Sarah was ninety, God told them that they would have a son. The Lord instructed Abraham and Sarah to name this child Isaac. He also promised them that He would bless their descendents through Isaac (Gen. 17:15–21). At the appointed time, Isaac was born to the two grateful parents (21:1–8). Sometime during Isaac's teenage years, God commanded Abraham, " 'Take now your son, your only son, whom you love, Isaac, and go to the land of Moriah; and offer him there as a burnt offering on one of the mountains of which I will tell you' " (22:2). Words cannot adequately express the anguish Abraham must have felt when he heard those words. Indeed, he was so disturbed that he "rose early in the morning" (probably indicating a sleepless night) and made all the travel preparations himself instead of delegating the job to his servants—another sign of his restlessness

(v. 3). Then he took Isaac and two of his servants and began the arduous three-day journey to Moriah. When Abraham saw the place where he was to sacrifice his son, he told his servants to wait for him and Isaac to return (v. 5). Then "Abraham took the wood of the burnt offering and laid it on Isaac his son [a burden suitable for an adolescent, not a young boy], and he took in his hand the fire and the knife" (v. 6a). As father and son hiked up the mountain together, Isaac asked Abraham, " 'Behold, the fire and the wood, but where is the lamb for the burnt offering?' " (vv. 6–7). We can infer from Isaac's question that he had witnessed and taken part in numerous sacrifices to God, which shows that Abraham had taught him much about the Lord. Yet, at this juncture, Abraham did not tell Isaac that *he* was to be the sacrifice. Perhaps Abraham was still hoping that God would provide an alternative sacrifice (v. 8). We go on to read that when "they came to the place of which God had told him . . . Abraham built the altar there, and arranged the wood, and bound his son Isaac, and laid him on the altar on top of the wood. And Abraham stretched out his hand, and took the knife to slay his son" (vv. 9–10). This account does not suggest any reluctance on Isaac's part. He was willing to obey his father and trust in God even if it meant risking his life. Are you prepared to risk as much?

B. Samuel. After Samuel was born to Elkanah and Hannah, he was raised by a judge and priest named Eli (1 Sam. 1:1–2:11, 4:18b). Although Eli was a busy and highly respected man in Israel, he had two sons of his own who publicly abused their priestly profession and rebelled against their father's counsel (2:12–17, 22–25). As if this were not enough, there is evidence that Eli encouraged the wickedness of his sons by failing to strongly rebuke them and by partaking of the sacrificial meat they were stealing (v. 29; 4:18b, which indicates that Eli was overweight).[1] Samuel was raised in the midst of this carnality. The text informs us that during a period when "word from the Lord was rare . . . [and] visions were infrequent," God called young Samuel, and he listened intently (3:1–18). Samuel was sensitive to the Lord. He did not allow his home situation to move him from his spiritual moorings (vv. 19–20). Are you open to God's call? Are you trying to live your life His way regardless of your circumstances?

C. Josiah. Prior to Josiah's reign over Judah, there ruled two wicked kings: Manasseh and Amon. Manasseh became king when he was twelve years old and "reigned fifty-five years in Jerusalem"

1. For more on Eli and his home see "Danger Signals of a Disintegrating Family," by Chuck Swindoll, in *Insights* (Winter 1984), pp. 21–25.

(2 Chron. 33:1). During his rule, "he did evil in the sight of the Lord according to the abominations of the nations whom the Lord dispossessed before the sons of Israel" (v. 2; cf. vv. 3–9). After he died, his son Amon became king at twenty-two years of age (vv. 20–21a). His two-year reign was marked by the same sins which were committed by his father, except that Amon never repented of his evil (vv. 21b–23; cf. vv. 10–16). After Amon was assassinated by his own servants, his son Josiah ascended to the throne in Jerusalem (vv. 24–25). Josiah was only "eight years old when he became king, and he reigned thirty-one years" (34:1). Unlike his father and grandfather, Josiah "did right in the sight of the Lord, and walked in the ways of his father David and did not turn aside to the right or to the left" (v. 2). We read that at age sixteen "he began to seek the God of his father David" (v. 3a). At age twenty "he began to purge Judah and Jerusalem" of everything that was being used for idol worship (vv. 3b–7). By age twenty-six, Josiah commissioned that the temple of God be repaired and the worship of the Lord be restored (34:8–35:19). This king stood by his convictions and brought an entire nation back to spiritual health. Now that's integrity! Are you that committed to God? Are you willing to live by your Christian beliefs regardless of the actions of others and the times in which you live?

D. Daniel. Another teenager who rose to the challenges of his day was Daniel. After the nation of Judah had fallen and the Jews had been taken to Babylon as slaves (586 B.C.), the Babylonian king Nebuchadnezzar "ordered Ashpenaz, the chief of his officials," to teach certain Jews "the literature and language of the Chaldeans" (Dan. 1:1–4). Along with their three-year education, the Jews were to receive "a daily ration from the king's choice food and from the wine which he drank" (v. 5). Daniel was among this select number of Jews (v. 6). But he "made up his mind that he would not defile himself" by eating the king's food and drinking his wine (v. 8a). So Daniel approached the individual who was responsible for his particular group and asked the man to give them only "'vegetables to eat and water to drink'" (vv. 11–12). The Babylonian official granted Daniel's request. And God abundantly blessed Daniel's faithfulness to Him (vv. 14–20). Are you willing to stand up for God? Are you prepared to withstand the pressure to compromise God's standard?

III. A Final Thought

Isaac, Samuel, Josiah, and Daniel were adolescents that did great things for God. Not all of these teenagers had godly parents, but all of them walked faithfully with God. If you are a parent, are you helping your children grow in their faith? They need you to be a spiritual model if they are to have the best opportunity to become obedient servants of the Lord. For godly character does not just happen; it is cultivated. Will you begin today to be a positive force in your children's spiritual development?

Living Insights

Study One

Adolescence isn't all bad . . . in fact, this study has helped us see what's good about it. Let's spend some extra time examining the scriptural examples of godly adolescents.

- The following chart summarizes the teaching in this lesson. Let's return to the passages listed and study them in more depth. You may choose to analyze one of these passages . . . or all four. The key is to go beyond what we looked at together and make some discoveries of your own.

Names	Scriptures	Tests	Strengths
Isaac	Genesis 22	To obey his father regardless of the cost	Willingness to risk
Samuel	1 Samuel 3	To mature spiritually in a carnal environment	Sensitivity to God
Josiah	2 Chronicles 34	To reign righteously in the midst of political and religious corruption	Commitment to integrity
Daniel	Daniel 1	To resist the pressure to compromise	Determination to stand

Living Insights

Study Two

We learned in this study that adolescents aren't always unwise and immature. Frankly, even those of us who are adults can learn some valuable lessons from the young lives of Isaac, Samuel, Josiah, and Daniel. Use the following questions to help stimulate your thinking in this area.

- Which of these four adolescents reminds you most of yourself?
- Which one is least like you?
- Can you relate to the tests these adolescents faced?
- What could you begin doing to further develop the strengths mentioned in this study?
- How could a close friend help you in any of these areas?

Reasons We Resist Becoming Mature

Hebrews 2–5

Most children are in a hurry to grow up. And even adults look forward to gaining more wisdom and sharpening their skills as they advance in age. Unfortunately, this drive for maturity seldom occurs in the spiritual realm. Rather than chart a course for the challenging waters of Christian adulthood, we often steer our lives close to the shorelines of spiritual childhood and adolescence. Although this is a safer course to navigate, it is not the one God wants for us. His desire is that we first prepare for the risks, responsibilities, and rewards of adulthood and then set sail for maturity with Him at the helm of our lives. Since this is God's will for us, why do we resist growing up in our faith? How can we cooperate with His plan for our full maturity in Christ? Some answers to these questions are found in Hebrews 2–5. We would be wise to listen to the message of this passage and heed its instruction.

I. A Time for Honest Confession

Before turning to the Book of Hebrews, let's consider three statements that, unfortunately, apply to most of us. Only by confessing their relevance to our lives will we be able to press on to maturity.

A. We are creatures of habit. Change—even if it is for our own good—makes us feel uncomfortable. Because of this, we cling to what is safe and familiar and resist that which is risky and new.

B. We want a Savior, not a Master. We find solace in our salvation, but we struggle with our sanctification. As C. S. Lewis says, "We want, in fact, not so much a Father in Heaven as a grandfather in heaven—a senile benevolence who, as they say, 'liked to see young people enjoying themselves,' and whose plan for the universe was simply that it might be truly said at the end of each day, 'a good time was had by all.' "[1]

C. We tend to stop short of our full potential. Rather than pursue what will stretch us, we often choose the path of least resistance. And we frequently rationalize our choices to do so by comparing ourselves with someone less mature or skillful. We seldom think about how we can reach beyond our present state toward greater Christlikeness.

II. A Letter with Relevant Information

Why do we continue to settle for second best in our relationship with God? Why don't we "[leave] the elementary teaching about the

1. C. S. Lewis, *The Problem of Pain* (New York: Macmillan Publishing Co., 1962), p. 40.

Christ, [and] press on to maturity"? (Heb. 6:1a). The Book of Hebrews reveals at least four reasons for spiritual laziness. This New Testament letter confronts the issue because its original readers were perilously close to rejecting Christianity and returning to their old belief-system.[2] Although many of us may not be in danger of turning our backs on Christ, we all can learn a great deal from this epistle about why believers resist growing up. With this in mind, let's consider what the text teaches.

A. We resist becoming mature because we drift away from what we have heard. The Greek word translated *drift away* in Hebrews 2:1 was often used to describe what happens to a ship that has been allowed to float away from its moorings. New Testament scholar Philip Hughes explains what this word conveys:

> The metaphor in mind here seems to be that of allowing the current to carry one away from a fixed point through carelessness and unconcern, and, instead of keeping a firm grip on the truth, of failing to maintain a secure anchorage which will keep one from drifting from the gospel. The imagery may well be related to that of [Hebrews] 6:19, where our author speaks of the Christian hope as a "sure and steadfast anchor of the soul." Those to whom this letter is addressed are evidently not far from losing their right to be acknowledged as authentic Christians because of a loss of nerve, a failure of application, or . . . a "wilful negligence" in practicing the faith they profess.[3]

The original recipients of this letter were compromising their Christian faith partially because of the persecution they had already suffered and the increased hardship they anticipated (10:32–36, 12:1–4, 13:3). Are you confronting challenging

2. Bible scholars are generally agreed that the original recipients of the Book of Hebrews were in danger of turning away from Christ by exalting other beings and revelations to a status equal to or higher than Christ's. However, scholars widely disagree as to the identity of this rival philosophical or religious system. If you would like to explore this issue, we recommend that you consult these sources: *Christianity and the Hellenistic World,* by Ronald H. Nash, Christian Free University Curriculum (Grand Rapids: Zondervan Publishing House; Dallas: Probe Ministries International, 1984), chap. 6; *New Testament Introduction,* by Donald Guthrie, 3d ed., rev. ed. (Downers Grove: InterVarsity Press, 1970), pp. 698–710; "The First Readers of Hebrews," by John V. Dahms, *Journal of the Evangelical Theological Society* 20:4 (December 1977), pp. 365–75; "Recent Contributions to the Understanding of Hebrews," by F. F. Bruce, *The Expository Times* 80 (October 1968–September 1969), pp. 260–64.

3. Philip Edgcumbe Hughes, *A Commentary on the Epistle to the Hebrews* (Grand Rapids: William B. Eerdmans Publishing Co., 1977), pp. 73–74.

situations with your eyes fixed on Christ, or are you capitulating your convictions with your heart set on human acceptance?

B. **We resist becoming mature because we fall away from the truth.** The writer of Hebrews states: "Take care, brethren, lest there should be in any one of you an evil, unbelieving heart, in falling away from the living God. But encourage one another day after day, as long as it is still called 'Today,' lest any one of you be hardened by the deceitfulness of sin" (3:12–13). Because the author refers to his original readers as brethren, we can conclude that he believed they were Christians (cf. 3:1, 10:19). It is also clear that the writer believed that once someone was saved by faith, he or she was forever secure in Christ (5:9, 7:25).[4] Given these facts, we can see that the phrase "falling away from the living God" (3:12b) could not refer to the loss of salvation. However, it does indicate that believers who habitually disobey God will lose some of the *benefits* of salvation. For example, most of the believing Israelites who were part of the Exodus were not allowed to enter Canaan—the Promised Land—because they constantly questioned God's faithfulness (vv. 8–11, 15–19; cf. Num. 14:22–38).[5] As believers today, we may experience discontentment, anxiety, sickness, a shortened life span, and the loss of everlasting rewards by becoming callous to the Lord's Word (see Acts 5:1–6; 1 Cor. 3:10–15, 11:18–34). However, when we seek to live our lives in obedience to God by the power of the Holy Spirit, we will receive the many blessings the Lord desires to give us (Pss. 84:11, 103:2–5; 1 Cor. 2:9; Phil. 4:19; 2 Pet. 1:3–4; Rev. 2:10). Are you sensitive to God, or has a sinful lifestyle hardened your heart against Him?

C. **We resist becoming mature because we fail to mix faith with truth.** Consider these words of exhortation and warning: "Therefore, let us fear lest, while a promise remains of entering His rest, any one of you should seem to have come

4. Some students of the Bible argue that Hebrews 6:1–8 teaches that Christians can lose their salvation. But this interpretation has several problems. First, as already noted, it contradicts what the writer of Hebrews says in other portions of his letter. Second, it is contrary to what Jesus taught about salvation (John 5:24, 6:37, 10:26–30). Third, if this interpretation is correct, then once salvation is lost, it cannot be regained (Heb. 6:6)—a conclusion that these exegetes generally do not want to accept. And fourth, this position displays a misunderstanding of the analogy given by the writer of Hebrews. He says that the fruit (works), not roots (salvation), of a Christian's life will be burned up if he or she is habitually disobedient (6:7–8; see also 1 Cor. 3:12–15, and "Hebrews," by Zane C. Hodges, in *The Bible Knowledge Commentary: New Testament Edition,* edited by John F. Walvoord and Roy B. Zuck [Wheaton: Victor Books, 1983], pp. 794–96).

5. For more information on some of the events leading to the Exodus, the Exodus itself, and major situations that followed, see the study guide titled *Moses: God's Man for a Crisis,* edited by Bill Watkins, from the Bible-teaching ministry of Charles R. Swindoll (Fullerton: Insight for Living, 1985).

short of it. For indeed we have had good news preached to us, just as [the Israelites did]; but the word they heard did not profit them, because it was not united by faith in those who heard" (Heb. 4:1–2). The Israelites heard God's promise about the rich and fertile land He was going to give them. But the Lord's Word brought no lasting spiritual change in their lives because they did not place their trust in it. The same tragedy occurs today. Each time we hear God's counsel and fail to make it a part of our lives, we defeat its purpose—to renew our lives into Christ's image (Rom. 8:28–29, 12:1–2; Col. 3:10–11). Do you trust that the Lord will do what He says? Do you believe in His counsel enough to apply it consistently to your life? Or are you just listening to His Word while living out your days as you please?

D. We resist becoming mature because we have become dull of hearing. The author of Hebrews points this out as well:

> Concerning him we have much to say, and it is hard to explain, since you have become dull of hearing. For though by this time you ought to be teachers, you have need again for someone to teach you the elementary principles of the oracles of God, and you have come to need milk and not solid food. For everyone who partakes only of milk is not accustomed to the word of righteousness, for he is a babe. But solid food is for the mature, who because of practice have their senses trained to discern good and evil. (Heb. 5:11–14)

The recipients of this letter had become slack and inattentive with regard to the Christian faith. As a result, they were still spiritual babes, even though enough time had elapsed for them to have become mature. How long have you been a Christian? Have you been partaking of the proper nourishment for spiritual growth? Are you receptive to the Scriptures, or do you spurn their application to your life?

III. A Word of Specific Application

We can restate the essence of what we have learned in this lesson with one positive principle: *The key to becoming spiritually mature is to remain teachable.* This applies to whatever situation we find ourselves in. Whether we experience gains or losses, honors or humiliations, joys or sorrows . . . the Lord can use them all to move us toward godliness if we will only trust Him and obey His Word. Of course, we often wish that God would leave us alone. After all, the road to holiness is difficult and often painful. But, as C. S. Lewis points out, the Lord loves us too much to abandon His perfecting work in our lives:

> We are, not metaphorically but in very truth, a Divine work of art, something that God is making, and therefore something with which He will not be satisfied until it has a certain character. . . . Over a sketch made idly to amuse a child, an artist may not take much trouble: he may be content to let it go even though it is not exactly as he meant it to be. But over the great picture of his life—the work which he loves, though in a different fashion, as intensely as a man loves a woman or a mother a child—he will take endless trouble—and would, doubtless, thereby *give* endless trouble to the picture if it were sentient. One can imagine a sentient picture, after being rubbed and scraped and re-commenced for the tenth time, wishing that it were only a thumb-nail sketch whose making was over in a minute. In the same way, it is natural for us to wish that God had designed for us a less glorious and less arduous destiny; but then we are wishing not for more love but for less.[6]

Living Insights

Study One

Methods of Bible study such as observing, interpreting, and applying the truths of Scripture can help change our lives. Another aspect of studying Scripture that can aid our growth is *correlating.* By this method we seek to understand how different verses on related topics fit together. Let's work on our correlation skills as we do the exercise below.

- The following chart lists the four primary references from Hebrews that were used in this lesson. What is the main idea of each passage? How do the central ideas fit together? How do the contexts of these passages help you see the relation between their main teachings? Read through Hebrews 2–5 and try your hand at correlating its concepts.

Continued on next page

6. Lewis, *Problem of Pain,* pp. 42–43.

Hebrews 2:1–3
Main Idea: Correlating Thought:
Hebrews 3:12–13
Main Idea: Correlating Thought:
Hebrews 4:1–2
Main Idea: Correlating Thought:
Hebrews 5:11–14
Main Idea:

Living Insights

Study Two

Our final point in this lesson was: The key to becoming spiritually mature is to remain teachable. Allow the following series of questions to help you personalize this truth.

—Do you consider yourself teachable?
—What has God been teaching you recently?
—What circumstances have spurred you on to maturity?
—Do you occasionally suffer from "dullness of hearing"?
—How does your "hearing" relate to your spiritual growth?
—Do you have a good mixture of faith and truth?
—Under what circumstances do you have the tendency to drift?
—What specific steps can you take to keep pressing on toward maturity?

The Church: Who Needs It?

Selected Scripture

While growing up in their faith, believers often go through periods in which they resent their church and even ignore its needs. Some Christians, however, go to the extreme of believing that their church is better than anyone else's. These individuals virtually worship their local assembly. Although both of these attitudes are common, neither represents a healthy view of the church. As we press on toward maturity, we need to realize the important role a local body of believers plays in our lives and consider how we should contribute to the church's effectiveness. We can start to accomplish this by taking a close look at what Scripture teaches about the universal and local church. Although we cannot cover all of the relevant passages, this lesson will help us get a handle on some of the more prominent ones. But first, let's briefly explore some of the varied opinions people have about the church.

I. People's Comments about the Local Church

When people talk about the local church, their comments can generally be grouped under three categories: identity, criticism, and expectation. Let's take a look at what is often said under each category.

A. Identity of the local church. Some people think of the local church as a business, an evangelistic center, a spiritual hospital, or a social club. Others see it as just a nice addition to the community.

B. Criticisms of the local church. Some critics of the local assembly charge that the church is the only organization that shoots its wounded. Many also accuse the church of being too narrow-minded and legalistic. However, others insist that it is not restrictive enough. Another criticism is that the church is only interested in collecting and spending its members' money rather than seeking to meet their needs. Many people also think that local congregations are filled with proud, hypocritical individuals who look down on those who do not attend a church.

C. Expectations of the local church. Local assemblies are exhorted by many to take public stands on moral and political issues, while being urged by others to stay out of the marketplace and stick to "spiritual matters." Some people think that effective ministry can only take place in a church that remains numerically small, while many believe that large assemblies can accomplish more than small ones.

II. Christ's Statement on the Church

Although human opinion about the local church varies and conflicts, God's Word on the subject does not. The Bible makes it clear that congregations are like a family.[1] The Scriptures also record that Jesus Christ is personally involved in the development and survival of the Church universal. Notice what He said: " 'I . . . say to you that you are Peter [which literally means "a rock"], and upon this rock I will build My church; and the gates of Hades shall not overpower it' " (Matt. 16:18). These words reveal at least three truths about the worldwide Body of Christ. First, *Christ is the Builder of the Church.* He designed it, and He provides the materials for its construction. It is His project from start to finish. Second, *Christ is the Owner of the Church.* Because He purchased it with His own blood (Acts 20:28b), it belongs to Him alone. Third, *Christ guarantees the survival of the Church.* No physical or spiritual force will ever defeat or destroy the Body of Christ. One comforting facet of these truths is that we who are Christians became members of the Lord's universal Church when we accepted Christ as our Savior. Therefore, we are a part of a huge congregation of believers that will ultimately be victorious over any and all enemies.

III. Paul's Commitment to the Church

Just as newborns require a family environment for proper development, so we need a local body of Christians who will help us mature in the Lord. The Apostle Paul affirms this truth throughout his many epistles. Let's consider some of what he says on this subject.

A. Romans 12:4–13. In these verses Paul explains how we should conduct ourselves in the local church so as to build healthy relationships. He exhorts us to use our spiritual gifts to serve one another (vv. 6–8). He also encourages us to exercise love "without hypocrisy" and to "abhor what is evil" while "[clinging] to what is good" (v. 9). To this he adds, "Be devoted to one another in brotherly love; give preference to one another in honor; not lagging behind in diligence, fervent in spirit, serving the Lord; rejoicing in hope, persevering in tribulation, devoted to prayer, contributing to the needs of the saints, practicing hospitality" (vv. 10–13). In short, the local church should be a source of commitment, accountability, and caring which arises from a familial bond in Christ. We all need to be a part of such a family.

B. 1 Corinthians 12:24b–26. In these verses Paul zeros in on the unity, compassion, and encouragement that characterize godly churches. Consider his words: "God has so composed the body, giving more abundant honor to that member which lacked, that there should be no division in the body, but that the members should have the same care for one another. And if one

1. Support for this statement can be found in the lesson in this study guide titled "Ages and Stages of Growing Up."

member suffers, all the members suffer with it; if one member is honored, all the members rejoice with it." We need local assemblies that will provide this kind of camaraderie.

C. 2 Corinthians 8:1–11, 9:6–8. The Apostle also affirms that churches are to be marked by generous financial involvement in the work of ministry. He conveys this in 2 Corinthians by first pointing out how willingly and liberally the churches of Macedonia supported the Jerusalem believers by their giving (8:1–4). Then he uses this example of generosity to encourage the Corinthian Christians to participate financially in the same cause (vv. 6–11). Finally, Paul states a principle and links it with an exhortation and a promise that apply to all generations of believers:

> He who sows sparingly shall also reap sparingly; and he who sows bountifully shall also reap bountifully. Let each one do just as he has purposed in his heart; not grudgingly or under compulsion; for God loves a cheerful giver. And God is able to make all grace abound to you, that always having all sufficiency in everything, you may have an abundance for every good deed. (9:6–8)

We need to support generously with our finances the congregation in which we are involved.

D. Galatians 5:1, 13–15. Local churches are also exhorted to encourage creativity and freedom. The theological basis for this is our salvation in Christ: "It was for freedom that Christ set us free [from sin]; therefore keep standing firm and do not be subject again to a yoke of slavery" (v. 1). Paul goes on to say that our freedom is not to be turned "into an opportunity for the flesh" but used for "[serving] one another" through love (v. 13b). "For the whole Law is fulfilled in one word, in the statement, 'You shall love your neighbor as yourself' " (v. 14). Unfortunately, some Christians misuse their freedom in Christ, viewing it as an excuse for tearing down fellow believers (v. 15a). But this is not what God desires. His will is that churches promote the full and spontaneous exercise of Christian freedom in the accomplishment of His work through love. All of us need an environment like this in which we can grow up God's way.

IV. Our Involvement in the Church

It is important for us to be part of a local church. Indeed, we need to "consider how to stimulate one another to love and good deeds, not forsaking our own assembling together, as is the habit of some, but encouraging one another; and all the more, as [we] see the day drawing near" (Heb. 10:24–25). How can we nurture one another toward godliness, help our churches become vital forces in the world, and glorify the Lord through it all? By taking on adult responsibilities in the local church. This involves at least eight tasks. Will you commit yourself to making them a part of your life?

A. We need to assume responsibility for our own spiritual nourishment by engaging in personal and corporate Bible study and prayer.

B. We need to participate in worship services on a regular basis.

C. We need to join in the "body life" of our churches in a congregational and small group context.

D. We need to exercise our spiritual gifts in appropriate areas of ministry.[2]

E. We need to support the numerous ministries of our churches through prayer and service.

F. We need to contribute financially to our churches in a consistent, generous manner.

G. We need to share our faith and support those who proclaim the gospel in other parts of the world.

H. We need to respond positively to the leadership of our churches in areas of ecclesiastical policy and discipline.

Living Insights

Study One

This lesson addresses one of the key questions in our world today: Who needs the local church? In answering this question, we learned some of the reasons why believers need to be part of a congregation. Let's look for more reasons to include on our list.

- The letter to the Ephesians reads like a treatise on the purpose and value of the local church. Copy the chart from the following page and read through the six chapters of this epistle. When you have finished reading Paul's letter, you should be able to give some more reasons the local church is so vitally important to Christians and to God's plan for the world.

2. If you would like to learn more about spiritual gifts, we suggest that you consult the following sources: Ronald E. Baxter, *The Gifts of the Spirit* (Grand Rapids: Kregel Publications, 1983); Rick Yohn, *Discover Your Spiritual Gift and Use It* (Wheaton: Tyndale House Publishers, 1974); Kenneth Cain Kinghorn, *Discovering Your Spiritual Gifts: A Personal Inventory Method* (Grand Rapids: Francis Asbury Press, 1981).

The Church: Why Do We Need It?	
References in Ephesians	Reasons

Living Insights

Study Two

Who needs the church? We do! This study requires us to step back and take a serious look at our level of commitment to the church.

- How involved are you in your local church? In your notebook, write down an honest appraisal of your present participation. Use the tasks listed under outline point IV in this lesson as a guideline for this exercise.

My Church Involvement

A Story for Adults to Remember

2 Samuel 24:8–25

Among the numerous Old Testament narratives, there are enlightening stories of ecstasy and triumph as well as agony and tragedy. Some of the most moving accounts concern the great Israelite king, David. One of these serves as a vivid illustration of several marks of spiritual maturity. Consequently, it seems fitting that we blow the dust off this ancient account and consider what it teaches us about growing up in God's family.

I. The Reason for Old Testament Stories

It is unfortunate that many contemporary Christians do not see the relevance of the Old Testament to their spiritual development. This opinion was certainly not held by the first-century Church. Indeed, the Apostle Paul affirms the value of the Old Testament in several of his letters. For example, in 2 Timothy 3:16–17 he writes, "All Scripture is inspired by God and profitable for teaching, for reproof, for correction, for training in righteousness; [so] that the man of God may be adequate, equipped for every good work." When Paul penned these words, he probably had in his possession few, if any, of the books that make up the New Testament. Therefore, the Scripture he had in mind was doubtless the thirty-nine books of the Old Testament. In another letter Paul states, "Whatever was written in earlier times [a reference to the Old Testament] was written for our instruction, that through perseverance and the encouragement of the Scriptures we might have hope" (Rom. 15:4). Here we learn that the Old Testament was composed and preserved "for our instruction." Certainly, this section of the Bible helped those saints who lived before the writing of the New Testament, but it was also designed to aid our walk with God. How does the Old Testament do this? It does so in at least three ways. First, it gives us *perseverance*—the ability to hold up under stress and endure trials. Second, it provides us with *encouragement.* The Old Testament helps us develop courage in our lives so that we can stand for what is right and become examples of spiritual stability. Third, the Old Testament gives us *hope*—the capability to remain faithful to God regardless of the circumstances. Given these truths, it seems safe to say that we will not become spiritually mature without a working knowledge and consistent application of Old Testament truths.

II. The Maturity of an Ancient King

The Old Testament book of 2 Samuel gives us insight into an aging King David. The Bible records that David was a faithful servant of God (1 Kings 14:8b), and yet it also reveals that he was a fallible human being. One of the wrongs he committed while king was to command that a census be taken of the nation of Israel (2 Sam. 24:1–2; cf. 1 Chron. 21:1).[1] This act was not inherently evil, but David's motives for doing it were. Apparently, David ordered this census to be taken because "he began to think more in terms of armaments and troops than in terms of the faithful mercies of God."[2] Old Testament scholar Gleason Archer explains:

> In his youth [David] had put his entire trust in God alone, whether he was facing Goliath with a slingshot or an army of Amalekites with a band of four hundred men. But in later years he had come to rely more and more on material resources, . . . and he learned to measure his strength by the yardstick of numbers and wealth.
>
> The Lord therefore decided that it was time for David to be brought to his knees once more and to be cast on the grace of God through a time of soul-searching trial. He therefore encouraged David to carry out the plan he had long cherished, that of counting up his manpower resources in order to plan his future military strategy with a view to the most effective deployment of his armies. Quite possibly this would also afford him a better base for assessment of taxes. And so God in effect said to him: "All right, go ahead and do it. Then you will find out how much good it will do you."[3]

It took "nine months and twenty days" to complete the census (2 Sam. 24:8b). The tally of the people revealed that "there were in Israel eight hundred thousand valiant men who drew the sword, and the men of Judah were five hundred thousand" (v. 9b). As the story unfolds, we find four characteristics of spiritual maturity illustrated in David's ensuing repentance.

A. A mature conscience. We read that "David's heart troubled him after he had numbered the people. So David said to the Lord, 'I have sinned greatly in what I have done. But now, O Lord, please take away the iniquity of Thy servant, for I have

1. Second Samuel 24:1 tells us that God's anger moved David to "number Israel and Judah." And 1 Chronicles 21:1 states that Satan provoked David to take a census. Some people maintain that these two passages contradict each other, but actually, they are compatible. In order to humble and strengthen David, the Lord encouraged him to command that a census be taken. Satan, however, became involved so he could deal a severe blow to both David and Israel. The Book of Job serves as another example of this kind of battle between God and Satan in the arena of human history. Gleason Archer gives a detailed discussion on this issue in his book *Encyclopedia of Bible Difficulties,* foreword by Kenneth S. Kantzer (Grand Rapids: Zondervan Publishing House, 1982), pp. 186–88.

2. Archer, *Bible Difficulties,* p. 187.

3. Archer, *Bible Difficulties,* p. 187.

acted very foolishly' " (v. 10). David did not try to rationalize his guilt. He recognized that his inner sense of grief was the result of sin. His sensitivity to God's righteous standard led him to face up to his wickedness and confess it before the Lord.

> ***Personal Application***
> As we grow in our relationship to the Lord, we must be willing to acknowledge our guilt and accept responsibility for our sinful actions.

B. A mature mind. We learn that "when David arose in the morning, the word of the Lord came to the prophet Gad, David's seer, saying, 'Go and speak to David' " (vv. 11–12a). The Lord commissioned Gad to lay three alternatives before the king, all of which were potential consequences of David's sin. They were (1) seven years of famine in Israel, (2) three months of running from his enemies, and (3) three days of pestilence in Israel (v. 13). Although David was allowed to choose his own punishment, he realized that the options he was offered would bring pain to others as well as to himself. We can see this truth unveiled in his response to Gad: " 'I am in great distress. Let us now fall into the hand of the Lord for His mercies are great, but do not let me fall into the hand of man' " (v. 14). It hurt David terribly to know that his wrong would impact his nation. But he wisely chose to place his fate and the fate of his country in the hands of the Lord rather than those of man.

> ***Personal Application***
> Even when confronted with God's discipline, we need to keep our minds focused on the Lord rather than on man. Moreover, we must learn to accept the consequences of our sins without expecting others to bail us out.

C. A mature attitude. In response to David's choice, "the Lord sent a pestilence upon Israel from the morning until the appointed time; and seventy thousand men of the people from Dan to Beersheba died" (v. 15). God's act of judgment greatly reduced the number of men that had been counted in David's census. And as the text points out, more would have been killed if the Lord had not stopped the angel from carrying out His command (v. 16). Apparently, God did so because of David's prayer: " 'Behold, it is I who have sinned, and it is I who have done wrong; but these sheep [the Israelites], what have they done? Please let Thy hand be against me and against my father's house' " (v. 17). After David's petition and the temporary cessation of God's judgment, "Gad came to David . . . and said to him, 'Go up, erect an altar to the Lord on the threshing floor of Araunah the Jebusite' " (v. 18). David obeyed without hesitation (v. 19). Now when Araunah saw the king of Israel coming toward him, he "went out and bowed his face to the ground before the king" (v. 20). David then told Araunah that he wanted to buy his threshing floor " 'in order to build an altar to the Lord, that the plague would be held back from the people' " (v. 21b). Araunah responded by trying to give David his entire livelihood without charge (vv. 22–24). "However, the king said to Araunah, 'No, but I will surely buy it from you for a price, for I will not offer burnt offerings to the Lord my God which cost me nothing.' So David bought the threshing floor and the oxen for fifty shekels of silver" (v. 24). David knew that he alone was responsible for his sin. He also understood that someone had to pay for it, and he was mature enough to accept the cost himself rather than try to charge it to someone else's account.

> ***Personal Application***
> We will never become spiritually mature until we decide to absorb the cost of our own actions. That is what personal responsibility involves—nothing less.

D. A mature spirit. The final scene in this story is one of Christlike humility. Before Araunah and some royal servants, "David built . . . an altar to the Lord, and offered burnt offerings and peace offerings. Thus the Lord was moved by entreaty for the land, and the plague was held back from Israel" (v. 25). David publicly bowed before God and, with a repentant heart, petitioned the Lord to end the plague.

> ***Personal Application***
> If we want to become godly adults, we must be willing to obey the Lord completely and humble ourselves before Him fully.

III. Some Lessons for Adults Today

As we reflect on this Old Testament story, we find woven throughout, three lessons on spiritual adulthood.

A. Regarding perseverance: When we fail, we do not quit.

B. Regarding encouragement: When we obey, we do not argue.

C. Regarding hope: When we sacrifice, we do not lose.

Continued on next page

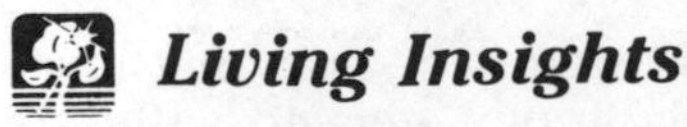

Living Insights

Study One

The Old Testament has been preserved for the purpose of instructing us in godliness and providing us with perseverance, encouragement, and hope. As we have seen, 2 Samuel 24 is a perfect illustration of these truths. Let's return to this passage and dig into it further.

- In an earlier Living Insights, we tried our hand at *paraphrasing*. Let's use this technique again in 2 Samuel 24:1–25. Remember, the purpose of this Bible study method is to bring out the feelings that are conveyed through the words of the account. Try to imagine yourself in the place of the biblical characters. This will help you get a handle on what they must have felt when they experienced sin, its consequences, and divine restoration.

Living Insights

Study Two

One trait that should characterize all adults is *maturity*. Unfortunately, many reach adult status in years without ever growing up in their character. The following questions are designed to stimulate your thinking with regard to maturity in adulthood. They can provide food for thought in your personal study or, better yet, be used as discussion starters with family members or a group of friends.

- How would you define *maturity?*
- What traits accompany maturity?
- Can you think of a particular time in your life when you first sensed that you were maturing? When was it?
- Is maturity something that can be taught? Why or why not?
- How do you view God's role in the maturing process?
- What are some passages of Scripture that are appropriate to this issue?

A Song for Adults to Sing

Psalm 26

The book of Psalms is the hymnal of the Old Testament. It is a treasurehouse of ancient songs, filled with the prayers and praises of God's people. These songs express a myriad of feelings—from intense joy to bitter sorrow. Indeed, virtually every human emotion is represented in the Psalter.[1] Although these hymns are available to all believers, some of them are geared primarily for spiritual adults. One such song is Psalm 26. In this passionate petition King David reveals an admirable level of maturity. Before beginning this study, take a few moments to read this Hebrew prayer. Then, as you return to the lesson, ask the Lord to help you make the message of this psalm a working part of your life.

I. A Song for the Mature

It's easy for even mature believers to act immaturely when they have been wronged. Disillusionment, resentment, and rage can take hold of believers if they respond inappropriately to being offended. David, the great Israelite king, knew this well. He spent many of his days running from a predecessor named Saul who, out of jealousy, wanted to kill him. Other people entered David's life from time to time, seeking selfish gain and pointing falsely accusing fingers. But more often than not, David kept his focus securely on God, trusting in Him for vindication and deliverance. Psalm 26 stands as an example of David's mature response to mistreatment. This song opens with a plea to the Lord that sets the stage for what follows. David cries out, "Vindicate me, O Lord, for I have walked in my integrity; / And I have trusted in the Lord without wavering" (v. 1). The Hebrew word translated *vindicate* conveys the idea of judging correctly in a court of law. As it is used in this psalm, the term can be rendered: "Execute judgment on my behalf." David appeals to God for justice because (1) he has acted with integrity in his relationships, and (2) he has "trusted in the Lord without wavering [literally, without sliding]." We do not know the particulars of the attack against David, but it is clear from the psalm that the charge was an unfair one. We learn from this ancient song how to handle mistreatment in a way that exhibits spiritual maturity. David communicates some counsel that will keep us on track in the midst of injustice if we will only heed it.

1. If you would like to learn more about the Psalms in order to unearth their gems of spiritual insight, we recommend that you consult the following sources: "Psalms," by Allen P. Ross, in *The Bible Knowledge Commentary: Old Testament Edition*, edited by John F. Walvoord and Roy B. Zuck (Wheaton: Victor Books, 1985), pp. 779–899; *A Christian Handbook to the Psalms*, by R. E. O. White (Grand Rapids: William B. Eerdmans Publishing Co.; Exeter: Paternoster Press, 1984); and two books by Derek Kidner: *Psalms 1–72* (Downers Grove: InterVarsity Press, 1973), and *Psalms 73–150* (Downers Grove: InterVarsity Press, 1975).

A. Be open before the Lord. David says, "Examine me, O Lord, and try me; / Test my mind and my heart" (v. 2). There are three key words in this verse. The first is the Hebrew term for *examine*, which means "scrutinize." Its use here communicates the idea of the Lord investigating and analyzing David's thoughts and motives (cf. Ps. 139:23–24a). The second key word is translated *try*, and it means "intensely prove." The term is rendered *testing* in Deuteronomy 8:2, where it refers to the many trials God put the Israelites through so that they would see their true characters and thereby be humbled. In Psalm 26, David petitions the Lord to expose and verify his true spiritual condition. The third Hebrew term, translated *test*, means "smelt, refine." It portrays metal being heated to a temperature hot enough to remove its impurities. By using this word, David is asking the Lord to remove any dross in his life through whatever method God deems best. We know from Scripture that the Lord's means of character-refining are often trials and tribulations. Such difficulties are never easy to endure, but they are always designed for our good. James 1:2–4 states this point well:

> When all kinds of trials and temptations crowd into your lives, my brothers, don't resent them as intruders, but welcome them as friends! Realise that they come to test your faith and to produce in you the quality of endurance. But let the process go on until that endurance is fully developed, and you will find you have become men of mature character, men of integrity with no weak spots.[2]

David wanted his life to be completely laid bare before God. So he requested that the Lord scrutinize his life, reveal his true condition, and purge any impurities from his character.

B. Remembering God's acceptance of you, continue to obey Him. When attacked unfairly, we are frequently tempted to doubt God's love for us and drift into disobedience. Realizing this, David recalls his experience of God's lovingkindness and his walk of obedience in God's truth (Ps. 26:3). David was committed to not allowing false accusations to get the best of him. So he focused his eyes on God's unfailing love and kept his feet walking down His righteous path.

C. Refuse to spend time with the wrong associates. Proof of David's faithfulness to the Lord is found in his refusal to "sit with deceitful men" and "go with pretenders" (v. 4). He reiterates this in these words: "I hate the assembly of evildoers, / And I will not sit with the wicked" (v. 5). David did not want evil people

2. J. B. Phillips, *The New Testament in Modern English*, rev. ed. (New York: The Macmillan Co., 1972), p. 478.

to influence his walk with God, so he spurned their counsel and even their company.[3]

D. Maintain a positive attitude. In contrast to associating with wicked individuals, David chose to worship in the sanctuary of the Lord. He says in his prayer, "I shall wash my hands in innocence, / And I will go about Thine altar, O Lord, / That I may proclaim with the voice of thanksgiving, / And declare all Thy wonders" (vv. 6–7). David decided to cope with unfair treatment by staying close to the Lord with a heart of purity and gratitude.

E. Be faithful in public worship. Even in the midst of personal assault, David could say, "O Lord, I love the habitation of Thy house, / And the place where Thy glory dwells" (v. 8). He did not avoid joining with God's people in worship. Instead, David sought out their company and drew from the Lord's strength in the sanctuary of Israel. The writer of Hebrews reminds us that we also should strive to meet regularly with other believers. Take a few moments to meditate on his exhortation: "Let us consider how to stimulate one another to love and good deeds, not forsaking our own assembling together, as is the habit of some, but encouraging one another" (Heb. 10:24–25a). Our commitment to public worship will not only express our devotion to God, it will strengthen our walk in righteousness even when the days are bleak.

F. Patiently stand and wait for relief. In the final section of Psalm 26, David makes it clear that he has no intention of taking justice into his own hands. He petitions the Lord to spare him from the common fate of "men of bloodshed" (Ps. 26:9). This is probably a reference to premature death. Then David reiterates his commitment to integrity and calls on God to deliver him from those who are falsely accusing him (v. 11). Lastly, in expectation of divine vindication, David says, "My foot stands on a level place; / In the congregations I shall bless the Lord" (v. 12). The Hebrew term for *level place* refers to a location that offers a commanding or panoramic view of an area. In this statement, David affirms that his perspective of his situation is the divine one. And because he sees his circumstances as God does, David can rest assured that the Lord will judge his case fairly and defend him fully.

3. We should not interpret this verse to mean that believers should never spend time with unbelievers. The Bible encourages us to develop relationships with non-Christians (Matt. 28:19; John 20:21–23; Acts 1:8, 8:26–40, 9:1–22). However, we should avoid those people who are genuine threats to the stability of our Christian faith (Rom. 16:17–18). For further discussion of this point, see the study guide titled *Relating to Others in Love: A Study of Romans 12–16*, edited by Bill Watkins, from the Bible-teaching ministry of Charles R. Swindoll (Fullerton: Insight for Living, 1985), pp. 65–68.

II. Some Characteristics of the Mature

A New Testament passage that sums up the main idea of Psalm 26 is 1 Peter 2:18–23.

> Servants, be submissive to your masters with all respect, not only to those who are good and gentle, but also to those who are unreasonable. For this finds favor, if for the sake of conscience toward God a man bears up under sorrows when suffering unjustly. For what credit is there if, when you sin and are harshly treated, you endure it with patience? But if when you do what is right and suffer for it you patiently endure it, this finds favor with God. For you have been called for this purpose, since Christ also suffered for you, leaving you an example for you to follow in His steps, who committed no sin, nor was any deceit found in His mouth; and while being reviled, He did not revile in return; while suffering, He uttered no threats, but kept entrusting Himself to Him who judges righteously.

From the teaching in these two biblical texts, we can identify three traits that characterize the spiritually mature Christian.

A. The mature believer wants to please God regardless of the cost or the circumstances.

B. The mature believer seeks to model the life of Christ.

C. The mature believer sees benefit, not just pain, in hardship.

Living Insights

Study One

The Psalms contain songs of encouragement for the believer committed to maturity. Their lyrics reflect the entire spectrum of human emotion. Psalm 26 is a prime example.

- After copying the following chart into your notebook, go back and carefully reread Psalm 26. Pick out twelve verbs that strike you as the most significant to the meaning of the psalm. In the next column write down why you feel they are significant. Then, with the help of a Bible dictionary, define each word. This process will deepen your understanding of the psalm's message and enhance its relevance to your life.

A Song for Adults to Sing—Psalm 26			
Verses	Verbs	Significance	Definitions

Living Insights

Study Two

As we worked through this series, we took a personal look at birth, infancy, childhood, and adolescence. The last stage we looked at was adulthood. Let's do some private reflection on our lives as adults.

- Copy the following chart into your notebook. Then fill in the blanks with answers that assess your spiritual maturity. Be honest. Use this as a time of review over some of the key areas of adult life.

Assessing My Own Adulthood
Areas of Adulthood: In what ways have I already grown up?
Areas of Need: In what ways do I still need to grow up?
Areas of Improvement: What strategy could I initiate for further growth?

Growing-up Goals for Diligent Disciples

Philippians 3:12–14, 2 Peter 1:1–11

We have seen in this series that God's goal for His people is spiritual maturity. And the only way we can reach this end is by passing through the stages of spiritual growth—birth, infancy, childhood, adolescence, and adulthood. Of course, we will never become fully mature until we are glorified. Then we will be like Christ in every aspect of our humanity (Rom. 8:28–30, 1 Cor. 15:50–57, 1 Thess. 5:23, Jude 24). But what should we do in the meantime? How should we live? How can we measure our maturity in Christ? The Apostle Peter's second letter provides us with succinct and realistic answers to these practical questions. As we examine the first eleven verses of this epistle, let's remain open to what the Holy Spirit has to reveal about our lives.

I. A Problem We All Face

We who are Christians know that Jesus Christ died for our sins and rose from the dead so that we could have abundant life. We also understand that the Holy Spirit was given to us so that we could have the power to be pleasing to God. Some Christians, however, think that truths like these guarantee that believers will never have struggles. Nothing could be farther from the truth! God's people have always gone through hard times, and they will continue to do so until God creates a new heaven and new earth (Rev. 20–22). But this fact should not dishearten us. Adversity is allowed by God to strengthen and purify us (James 1:2–4; 1 Pet. 2:18–23, 3:17–18, 4:12–19, 5:10). Indeed, God usually brings struggles into the lives of His people so that He can refine and reshape their characters. And He calls on us to learn from our trials so that we can grow into spiritually mature adults. The Apostle Paul displayed this teachability throughout his lifetime. Observe what he says:

> I have *learned* to be content in whatever circumstances I am. I know how to get along with humble means, and I also know how to live in prosperity; in any and every circumstance I have *learned* the secret of being filled and going hungry, both of having abundance and suffering need. (Phil. 4:11b–12, emphasis added)

Paul did not gain spiritual maturity without making sacrifices or going through a process of growth. Indeed, in the same letter he adds that he is still reaching for full Christian adulthood:

> Not that I have already obtained it, or have already become perfect, but I press on in order that I may lay hold of that for which also I was laid hold of by Christ

Jesus. Brethren, I do not regard myself as having laid hold of it yet; but one thing I do: forgetting what lies behind and reaching forward to what lies ahead, I press on toward the goal for the prize of the upward call of God in Christ Jesus. (3:12–14)

Therefore, since struggling is an integral part of the Christian life, we must come to grips with it so that we can grow.

II. A Plea for Balance and Obedience

Peter gives us some sound counsel on how we can mature consistently in our faith. Let's consider what he says.

A. Divine resources. One of the things we need to understand is what we have in Christ. Peter singles out three truths that all Christians can claim. First, we have "divine power [which] has granted to us everything pertaining to life and godliness, through the true knowledge of Him who called us by His own glory and excellence" (2 Pet. 1:3). Second, we have received God's "precious and magnificent promises" (v. 4a). And third, we have "become partakers of the divine nature," and thereby become recipients of the constant presence of God (v. 4b). Although these facts are important, they are insufficient to lead us to spiritual adulthood. What is the missing ingredient?

B. Human diligence. Spiritual maturity can only be attained when the principles and commands of Scripture are diligently obeyed (v. 5a). God has given us all we need to live a Spirit-filled, Christlike life. It is up to us to apply His resources His way . . . to exercise Christian responsibility in our walk with God.

III. Some Objectives for Devoted Disciples

What should the lifetime ambition of diligent disciples be? We know that the goal of Christian maturity is perfection. But we need to understand what constitutes Christian perfection. Once we do, we will have a spiritual yardstick by which we can measure our growth in Christ. In 2 Peter 1:5–7, we find such a standard. Let's consider each of its elements.

A. Faith. The foundation of the Christian life is faith in God (v. 5a). We must believe that what the Lord reveals is true, accept it as our standard for life, and act on it with confidence. To faith we are to "supply" seven other virtues. The term for this word was used in ancient Greece with reference to a director who paid the expenses for training a chorus. Eventually "the word came to be used of one who provides for or supports others or supplies something for them in abundance."[1] In other

1. Kenneth O. Gangel, "2 Peter," in *The Bible Knowledge Commentary: New Testament Edition*, edited by John F. Walvoord and Roy B. Zuck (Wheaton: Victor Books, 1983), p. 865. See also *A Linguistic Key to the Greek New Testament*, by Fritz Rienecker, edited by Cleon L. Rogers, Jr. (Grand Rapids: Zondervan Publishing House, 1980), p. 769.

words, to their faith, believers are to add lavishly the other essentials of Christian maturity that Peter mentions.

B. **Moral excellence.** One of the virtues Peter exhorts us to pursue is moral excellence (v. 5b). The Greek term he uses to communicate this quality refers to the proper fulfillment of something. For example, the purpose of many medicines is fulfilled when they facilitate healing. Spiritually, we fulfill our purpose when we conform ourselves to the holy character of Christ.

C. **Knowledge.** Another quality we should strive for is knowledge (v. 5c). The Greek term for this virtue does not refer primarily to intellectual pursuits but focuses essentially on the application of divine truth to life. This involves thinking and acting with discernment.

D. **Self-control.** The ability to maintain a grip on ourselves is another trait we should seek to develop (v. 6a). We must control our passions rather than allow them to master us.

E. **Perseverance.** To the other virtues, we need to add an abundance of perseverance (v. 6b). The Greek term for this character trait means "abiding under." Kenneth Gangel observes that "it is frequently used in the New Testament to refer to constancy or steadfast endurance under adversity, without giving in or giving up (cf. Rom. 5:3–4; 15:4–5; 2 Cor. 1:6, 6:4; Col. 1:11; 1 Thess. 1:3; 2 Thess. 1:4; James 1:3)."[2] We are to "hang tough" in our faith regardless of the circumstances.

F. **Godliness.** We are also to pursue true piety in our attitudes and actions (2 Pet. 1:6c). This quality has two dimensions: (1) a correct and sincere reverence toward God and (2) a faithful and humble service to others.

G. **Brotherly kindness.** In part, true godliness manifests itself in brotherly kindness—"a fervent practical caring for others" (v. 7a; cf. 1 John 3:16–18, 4:20).[3] This virtue cannot be obtained if we are untouchable and uncompassionate.

H. **Love.** The last quality Peter mentions is love—desiring and doing the greatest good for others (2 Pet. 1:7b). We can expand this definition by using an acrostic device that may help us remember and apply it.

L — listening when another person is speaking
O — overlooking petty faults and forgiving all failures
V — valuing other people for who they are
E — expressing love in practical ways

2. Gangel, "2 Peter," p. 866.

3. Gangel, "2 Peter," p. 866.

IV. A Fact, an Exhortation, and a Promise

In verses 8–11 of 2 Peter 1, the Apostle conveys a truth that is twofold. On the positive side, those of us who manifest the virtues listed and continue to grow in them are "neither useless nor unfruitful in the true knowledge of our Lord Jesus Christ" (v. 8). On the negative side, however, believers who do not have these qualities are "blind or short-sighted, having forgotten [their] purification from [their] former sins" (v. 9). These Christians choose to live spiritually immature lives rather than enjoy the abundant fruit of a righteous lifestyle. Based on this fact, Peter exhorts us to "be all the more diligent to make certain about [God's] calling and choosing you" (v. 10a). In other words, we are to see our spiritual growth as an indication of our salvation in Christ. Finally, Peter gives us a promise: "As long as you practice these [virtues], you will never stumble; for in this way the entrance into the eternal kingdom of our Lord and Savior Jesus Christ will be abundantly supplied to you" (vv. 10b–11).

V. A Suggestion to Remember and Apply

Many believers live as if they were victims, not victors, in Christ. If we believe that Christ has saved us from sin and that God has given us all the resources necessary to achieve spiritual adulthood, then we can live like overcomers, not down-and-outers. Are you a Christian? Then live like one in the power of the Holy Spirit. Blessed is the Christian who does what a Christian is supposed to do.

Continued on next page

Living Insights

Study One

Birth . . . infancy . . . childhood . . . adolescence . . . adulthood. We've looked at all the ages and stages of growing up in God's family. How well do you remember the key truths from this series? Let's conduct a brief review.

- Copy the following chart into your notebook. Using your Bible, notebook, and study guide, look for the most important *truth* you discovered in each lesson. Write it down in the right-hand column. We'll look at applications in the next study.

Growing Up in God's Family	
Lesson Titles	Key Truths
Analysis of a Crop Failure	
Ages and Stages of Growing Up	
Birth and Infancy: Operation Survival	
Let's Return to the Basics	
Look . . . I'm Walking!	
The Delights and Dangers of Childhood	
Adult Talk about "Childish Things"	
Three Proofs of Growth	
Adolescents in Adult Bodies	
When Peter Pan Comes to Church	
What's *Right* about Adolescence?	
Reasons We Resist Becoming Mature	
The Church: Who Needs It?	
A Story for Adults to Remember	
A Song for Adults to Sing	
Growing-up Goals for Diligent Disciples	

Living Insights

Study Two

Let's continue our review of the ages and stages of growing up. In this study we want to turn our attention toward the applications that have had the greatest effect on us.

- After you've copied the following chart into your notebook, repeat the process followed in the preceding exercise. However, this time look for the most important *application* in each lesson. Write it down in the right-hand column.

Growing Up in God's Family	
Lesson Titles	Key Applications
Analysis of a Crop Failure	
Ages and Stages of Growing Up	
Birth and Infancy: Operation Survival	
Let's Return to the Basics	
Look . . . I'm Walking!	
The Delights and Dangers of Childhood	
Adult Talk about "Childish Things"	
Three Proofs of Growth	
Adolescents in Adult Bodies	
When Peter Pan Comes to Church	
What's *Right* about Adolescence?	
Reasons We Resist Becoming Mature	
The Church: Who Needs It?	
A Story for Adults to Remember	
A Song for Adults to Sing	
Growing-up Goals for Diligent Disciples	

Books for Probing Further

Growing up in God's family is very much like growing up in a natural family. There are times when growth is easy and fun, and other occasions when it is difficult and painful. Whatever the experience, pursuing spiritual adulthood God's way brings great rewards and opportunities. Are you committed to growing up as a Christian? Do you want your faith to impact the lives of others in a positive way? If your answer is yes, you may be interested in probing further into some of the subjects dealt with in this study guide. With this in mind, we have compiled a bibliography of sources that can further aid your Christian growth. Our hope is that these books will help you better understand the Scriptures and apply them to your life.

I. Growing Up to Spiritual Adulthood

Bridges, Jerry. *The Practice of Godliness.* The Christian Character Library. Colorado Springs: NavPress, 1983.

Chafer, Lewis Sperry. *He That is Spiritual.* Rev. ed. Foreword by John F. Walvoord. Grand Rapids: Zondervan Publishing House, 1967.

Colson, Charles W. *Loving God.* Grand Rapids: Zondervan Publishing House, 1983.

Fleming, Jean. *Between Walden and the Whirlwind.* The Christian Character Library. Colorado Springs: NavPress, 1985.

Hocking, David. *Are You Spirit-filled?* Eugene: Harvest House Publishers, 1985.

Knowles, Andrew. *Real-life Christianity.* A Lion Manual. Belleville: Lion Publishing Corp., 1984. Designed specifically for teenagers.

MacDonald, Gordon. *Ordering Your Private World.* Nashville: Thomas Nelson Publishers, 1984.

Nystrom, Carolyn. *Growing Jesus' Way.* Illustrated by Wayne A. Hanna. Children's Bible Basics. Chicago: Moody Press, 1982.

Packer, J. I. *Keep in Step with the Spirit.* Old Tappan: Fleming H. Revell Co., 1984.

Peace, Richard. *Pilgrimage: A Handbook on Christian Growth.* Reprint. Foreword by Lyman Coleman. Grand Rapids: Baker Book House, 1984.

Sanders, J. Oswald. *Enjoying Intimacy with God.* Foreword by J. I. Packer. Chicago: Moody Press, 1980.

Swindoll, Charles R. *Integrity: The Mark of Godliness.* Portland: Multnomah Press, 1981.

———. *Strengthening Your Grip: Essentials in an Aimless World.* Waco: Word Books, 1982.

———. *Victory: A Winning Game Plan for Life.* Lifemaps series. Waco: Word Books, 1984.

White, Jerry. *The Power of Commitment.* The Christian Character Library. Colorado Springs: NavPress, 1985.

White, John. *The Fight: A Practical Handbook for Christian Living.* Downers Grove: InterVarsity Press, 1976.

II. Growing Up in a Church Family

Berry, Jo. *Growing, Sharing, Serving.* Elgin: David C. Cook Publishing Co., 1979.

Bridges, Jerry. *True Fellowship.* The Christian Character Library. Colorado Springs: NavPress, 1985.

Crabb, Lawrence J., Jr., and Allender, Dan B. *Encouragement: The Key to Caring.* Grand Rapids: Zondervan Publishing House, 1984.

Doering, Jeanne. *Your Power of Encouragement.* Chicago: Moody Press, 1982.

Eims, LeRoy. *Disciples in Action.* Colorado Springs: NavPress; Wheaton: Victor Books, 1981.

———. *The Lost Art of Disciple Making.* Foreword by Robert E. Coleman. Grand Rapids: Zondervan Publishing House, 1978.

Getz, Gene A. *Serving One Another.* Wheaton: Victor Books, 1984.
———. *Sharpening the Focus of the Church.* Foreword by George W. Peters. Chicago: Moody Press, 1974.
Howard, J. Grant. *The Trauma of Transparancy: A Biblical Approach to Interpersonal Communication.* A Critical Concern Book. Portland: Multnomah Press, 1979.
Hull, Bill. *Jesus Christ Disciplemaker.* Colorado Springs: NavPress, 1984.
MacDonald, Gail and Gordon. *If Those Who Reach Could Touch.* Chicago: Moody Press, 1984.
McMinn, Gordon. *Choosing to Be Close: Fill Your Life with Rewarding Relationships.* With Larry Libby. Portland: Multnomah Press, 1984.
Mayhall, Jack. *Discipleship: The Price and the Prize.* Wheaton: Victor Books, 1984.
Nystrom, Carolyn. *What is a Church?* Illustrated by Wayne A. Hanna. Children's Bible Basics. Chicago: Moody Press, 1981.
Strauss, Richard. *Getting Along with Each Other.* San Bernardino: Here's Life Publishers, 1985.
Swindoll, Charles R. *Dropping Your Guard: The Value of Open Relationships.* Waco: Word Books, 1983.
———. *Improving Your Serve: The Art of Unselfish Living.* Waco: Word Books, 1981.
Wilke, Harold H. *Creating the Caring Congregation.* Foreword by Dr. Karl Menninger. Nashville: Abingdon Press, 1980.
Williams, June A. *Strategy of Service.* Ministry Resources Library. Grand Rapids: Zondervan Publishing House, 1984.

III. Growing Up through an Understanding of Scripture

Archer, Gleason L. *Encyclopedia of Bible Difficulties.* Foreword by Kenneth S. Kantzer. Grand Rapids: Zondervan Publishing House, 1982.
Barber, Cyril J. *Dynamic Personal Bible Study.* Foreword by Charles C. Ryrie. Neptune: Loizeaux Brothers, 1981.
Beitzel, Barry J. *The Moody Atlas of Bible Lands.* Chicago: Moody Press, 1985.
Bruce, F. F. *Abraham and David: Places They Knew.* Nashville: Thomas Nelson Publishers, 1984.
———. *Jesus and Paul: Places They Knew.* Nashville: Thomas Nelson Publishers, 1983.
Doney, Meryl. *How Our Bible Came to Us.* Illustrations by Peter Dennis. Belleville: Lion Publishing Corporation, 1985. Especially geared for older children and teenagers.
Ellisen, Stanley A. *Knowing God's Word.* Nashville: Thomas Nelson Publishers, 1984.
Fee, Gordon D., and Stuart, Douglas. *How to Read the Bible for All Its Worth: A Guide to Understanding the Bible.* Grand Rapids: Academie Books, Zondervan Publishing House, 1982.
Gaebelein, Frank E., ed. *The Expositor's Bible Commentary.* 12 vols. Grand Rapids: Regency Reference Library, Zondervan Publishing House, 1976–1985.
Geisler, Norman L., and Nix, William E. *From God to Us: How We Got Our Bible.* Chicago: Moody Press, 1974.
Henrichsen, Walter A. *A Layman's Guide to Interpreting the Bible.* Rev. and exp. ed. Grand Rapids: Zondervan Publishing House; Colorado Springs: NavPress, 1978.
Herr, Ethel L. *Bible Study for Busy Women.* Chicago: Moody Press, 1982.
The International Standard Bible Encyclopedia. 4 vols. Rev. ed. Grand Rapids: William B. Eerdmans Publishing Co., 1979, 1982, 1986.
Jenkins, Simon. *Bible Mapbook.* Belleville: Lion Publishing Corp., 1985.
Jensen, Irving L. *How to Profit from Bible Reading.* Chicago: Moody Press, 1985.
Mackowski, Richard M. *Jerusalem: City of Jesus.* Photography by Garo Nalbandian. Grand Rapids: William B. Eerdmans Publishing Co., 1980.

Mickelsen, A. Berkeley, and Mickelsen, Alvera M. *Understanding Scripture: A Laymen's* [sic] *Guide to Interpreting the Bible.* Ventura: Regal Books, 1982.
Millard, Alan. *Treasures from Bible Times.* Belleville: Lion Publishing Corp., 1985.
Nelson's Bible Encyclopedia for the Family. Nashville: Thomas Nelson Publishers, 1982.
The New International Dictionary of Biblical Archaeology. Grand Rapids: Regency Reference Library, Zondervan Publishing House, 1983.
Packer, J. I.; Tenney, Merrill C.; and White, William, Jr., eds. *The Bible Almanac.* Nashville: Thomas Nelson Publishers, 1980.
Richards, Lawrence O. *Expository Dictionary of Bible Words.* Grand Rapids: Regency Reference Library, Zondervan Publishing House, 1985.
Ryken, Leland. *The Literature of the Bible.* Grand Rapids: Zondervan Publishing House, 1974.
Shedd, Charlie and Martha. *Bible Study in Duet.* Grand Rapids: Pyranee Books, Zondervan Publishing House, 1984.
Sterrett, T. Norton. *How to Understand Your Bible.* Rev. ed. Downers Grove: InterVarsity Press, 1974.
Stott, John R. W. *Understanding the Bible.* Reprint. Glendale: Regal Books, 1973.
Tidball, Derek. *The Social Context of the New Testament: A Sociological Analysis.* Grand Rapids: Academie Books, Zondervan Publishing House, 1984.
Unger, Merrill F. *Unger's Bible Dictionary.* 3d ed., rev. Chicago: Moody Press, 1966.
Vine, W. E., et al, eds. *An Expository Dictionary of Biblical Words.* Rev. ed. Nashville: Thomas Nelson Publishers, 1985.
Vos, Howard F. *Archaeology in Bible Lands.* Chicago: Moody Press, 1977.
———. *An Introduction to Bible Geography.* Rev. ed. Chicago: Moody Press, 1983.
———. *Effective Bible Study: A Guide to Sixteen Methods.* Grand Rapids: Zondervan Publishing House, 1956.
Wald, Oletta. *The Joy of Discovery in Bible Study.* Rev. ed. Minneapolis: Augsburg Publishing House, 1975.
Walton, John H. *Chronological and Background Charts of the Old Testament.* Foreword by Merrill C. Tenney. Grand Rapids: Academie Books, Zondervan Publishing House, 1978.
Walvoord, John F., and Zuck, Roy B., eds. *The Bible Knowledge Commentary.* 2 vols. Wheaton: Victor Books, 1983, 1985.
Wiseman, Donald J., and Yamauchi, Edwin. *Archaeology and the Bible: An Introductory Study.* Grand Rapids: Zondervan Publishing House, 1979.
Wright, Chris. *User's Guide to the Bible.* A Lion Manual. Belleville: Lion Publishing Corp., 1984. Designed specifically for teenagers.
Wright, G. Ernest. *Biblical Archaeology.* Rev. ed. Philadelphia: The Westminster Press, 1962.

Insight for Living
Cassette Tapes
GROWING UP IN GOD'S FAMILY

How easy it is to think that getting older guarantees we're growing wiser. Not necessarily! Aging doesn't always result in maturity. So what is our need? To grow *up* in God's family. These sixteen lessons talk about trading in a passive, laid-back lifestyle for an active, on-target plan of growth.

			U.S.	Canadian
GUF	**CS**	**Cassette series—includes album cover . . . .**	**$ 44.50**	**$ 56.50**
		Individual cassettes—include messages A and B	**5.00**	**6.35**

These prices are effective as of February 1986 and are subject to change.

GUF 1-A: ***Analysis of a Crop Failure***—Mark 4:1–20
B: ***Ages and Stages of Growing Up***—Selected Scripture

GUF 2-A: ***Birth and Infancy: Operation Survival***—Selected Scripture
B: ***Let's Return to the Basics***—Selected Scripture

GUF 3-A: ***Look . . . I'm Walking!***—Romans 6:6–13, Ephesians 5:1–21
B: ***The Delights and Dangers of Childhood***—Selected Scripture

GUF 4-A: ***Adult Talk about "Childish Things"***—Selected Scripture
B: ***Three Proofs of Growth***—Matthew 10:1–10, Acts 4:32–37

GUF 5-A: ***Adolescents in Adult Bodies***—Selected Scripture
B: ***When Peter Pan Comes to Church***—1 Corinthians

GUF 6-A: ***What's* Right *about Adolescence?***—Selected Scripture
B: ***Reasons We Resist Becoming Mature***—Hebrews 2–5

GUF 7-A: ***The Church: Who Needs It?***—Selected Scripture
B: ***A Story for Adults to Remember***—2 Samuel 24:8–25, Romans 15:4

GUF 8-A: ***A Song for Adults to Sing***—Psalm 26
B: ***Growing-up Goals for Diligent Disciples***—Philippians 3:12–14, 2 Peter 1:1–11

Ordering Information

U.S. ordering information: You are welcome to use our toll-free number (for orders only) between the hours of 8:30 A.M. and 4:00 P.M., Pacific Time, Monday through Friday. We can accept only Visa or MasterCard when taking your order by phone. The number is (800) 772-8888. This number may be used anywhere in the continental United States excluding California, Hawaii, and Alaska. Orders from those areas are handled through our Sales Department at (714) 870-9161. We are unable to accept collect calls.

Your order will be processed promptly. We ask that you allow four to six weeks for delivery by fourth-class mail. If you wish your order to be shipped first-class, please add 10 percent of the total order (not including California sales tax) for shipping and handling.

Canadian ordering information: Your order will be processed promptly. We ask that you allow approximately four weeks for delivery by first-class mail to the U.S./Canadian border. All orders will be shipped from our office in Fullerton, California. For our listeners in British Columbia, a 7 percent sales tax must be added to the total of all tape orders (not including first-class postage). For further information, please contact our office at (604) 272-5811.

Payment options: We accept personal checks, money orders, Visa, and MasterCard in payment for materials ordered. Unfortunately, we are unable to offer invoicing or COD orders. If the amount of your check or money order is less than the amount of your purchase, your check will be returned so that you may place your order again with the correct amount. All orders must be paid in full before shipment can be made.

Returned checks: There is a $10 charge for any returned check (regardless of the amount of your order) to cover processing and invoicing.

Guarantee: Our tapes are guaranteed for ninety days against faulty performance or breakage due to a defect in the tape. For best results, please be sure your tape recorder is in good operating condition and is cleaned regularly.

Mail your order to one of the following addresses:

Insight for Living
Sales Department
Post Office Box 4444
Fullerton, CA 92634

Insight for Living Ministries
Post Office Box 2510
Vancouver, BC
Canada V6B 3W7

Quantity discounts and gift certificates are available upon request.

Overseas ordering information is provided on the reverse side of the order form.

Order Form

Please send me the following cassette tapes:

The current series: ☐ GUF CS Growing Up in God's Family

Individual cassettes: ☐ GUF 1 ☐ GUF 2 ☐ GUF 3 ☐ GUF 4
☐ GUF 5 ☐ GUF 6 ☐ GUF 7 ☐ GUF 8

I am enclosing:

$________ To purchase the cassette series for $44.50 (in Canada $56.50*) which includes the album cover

$________ To purchase individual tapes at $5.00 each (in Canada $6.35*)

$________ Total of purchases

$________ California residents please add 6 percent sales tax

$________ *British Columbia residents please add 7 percent sales tax

$________ Canadian residents please add 6 percent for postage

$________ U.S. residents please add 10 percent for first-class shipping and handling if desired

$________ **Overseas residents please add appropriate postage** (See postage chart under "Overseas Ordering Information.")

$________ As a gift to the Insight for Living radio ministry for which a tax-deductible receipt will be issued

$________ **Total amount due (Please do not send cash.)**

Form of payment:

☐ Check or money order made payable to Insight for Living

☐ Credit card (Visa or MasterCard only)

If there is a balance: ☐ Apply it as a donation ☐ Please refund

Credit card purchases:
☐ Visa ☐ MasterCard number ________
Expiration date ________
Signature ________
We cannot process your credit card purchase without your signature.

Name ________

Address ________

____

City ________

State/Province ________ Zip/Postal code ________

Country ________

Telephone (   ) ________ Radio station __ __ __ __

Should questions arise concerning your order, we may need to contact you.

Overseas Ordering Information

To ensure efficient processing of your request, please note the following information.

Estimated time of delivery: We ask that you allow approximately twelve to sixteen weeks for delivery by surface mail. If you would like your order sent airmail, the length of delivery may be reduced. All orders will be shipped from our office in Fullerton, California.

Payment options: Due to fluctuating currency rates, we can accept only personal checks made payable in U.S. funds, international money orders, Visa, and MasterCard in payment for materials ordered. If the amount of your check or money order is less than the amount of your purchase, your check will be returned so that you may place your order again with the correct amount. All orders must be paid in full before shipment can be made.

Returned checks: There is a $10 charge for any returned check (regardless of the amount of your order) to cover processing and invoicing.

Postage and handling: Please add to the amount purchased the basic postage cost for the service you desire. All orders must include postage based on the chart below.

Purchase Amount		Surface Postage	Airmail Postage
From	To	Percentage of Order	Percentage of Order
$ .01	$15.00	40%	75%
15.01	75.00	25%	45%
75.01	or more	15%	40%

Guarantee: Our tapes are guaranteed for ninety days against faulty performance or breakage due to a defect in the tape. For best results, please be sure your tape recorder is in good operating condition and is cleaned regularly.

Mail your order or inquiry to the following address:

Insight for Living
Sales Department
Post Office Box 4444
Fullerton, CA 92634

Quantity discounts and gift certificates are available upon request.